CW01668554

Anglesey Sketches

Margaret Hughes

illustrated by
N. Squire Johnson

GWASG
Carreg
Gwalch

© Text: Margaret Hughes

Copyright © by Gwasg Carreg Gwalch 1999
All rights reserved. No part of this publication
may be reproduced or transmitted, in any form
or by any means, without permission.

ISBN: 0-86381-540-5

Cover design: Alan Jones

First published in 1999 by Gwasg Carreg Gwalch,
12 Iard yr Orsaf, Llanrwst, Wales LL26 0EH
☎ *(01492) 642031*
Printed and published in Wales.

Margaret Hughes is a one-time advertising copywriter turned newspaper journalist. She was a staff reporter for Lancashire & Cheshire Newspapers, later working freelance to write for magazines and radio in the Manchester area. A Welsh speaker, she now lives in Anglesey.

For Emyr
– Er Cof

Thanks . . .

The author wishes to thank the Liverpool Daily Post, North Wales Newspapers, Country Quest and the Anglesey Antiquarian Society & Field Club for permission to use, or reproduce in edited form, articles which have appeared previously in their publications . . .

To Norman Squire Johnson, R.I.B.A. (retd.), for his evocative illustrations . . .

Also Anne Venables and staff at the County Archives office in Llangefni for unstinting support during research . . .

And to Dewi O. Jones, F.L.A., for his generous help in casting a critical eye over the manuscript.

Contents

Contents

First Impressions

Travelling by road along the expressway, which skirts the coast of North Wales, the first glimpse of Anglesey comes on emerging from the Penmaenbach tunnel when Ynys Seiriol (Puffin) and the lighthouse at Trwyn Penmon beckon across the wide mouth of the Menai Strait. If the weather is clear, the tantalising outline of the coastline to the north of the Strait promises joys to come.

The Strait narrows, with the vast golden extent of Traeth Lafan at low tide stretching across to the opposite shore at Beaumaris, which nestles into the hillside behind. At Abergwyngregyn, Anglesey is lost to view for a while as the Penrhyn estate and its massive castle interrupt, and it is not until the road crosses the Strait over the upper deck of the Britannia Bridge that the visitor sees the island again.

Train travellers have a similar introduction. The railway runs parallel to the expressway before plunging into two tunnels before Bangor station, and then into the Belmont tunnel at the far end. This brings the track close to the road for a glimpse of Menai Bridge town across the narrowed Strait, before it crosses to the island by the lower deck of the Britannia Bridge.

Visitors approaching from Porthmadog and the south have yet a different introduction. A gap in the hills south of Llanllyfni gives a sudden panoramic view of the western tip of Anglesey across Llanddwyn Bay. The coast beyond meanders into the distance towards the dramatic hump of Holyhead Mountain (only 220 metres high but appearing much higher because of the low-lying land in between). The road runs alongside the Strait from Caernarfon, with the green fields around Brynsiencyn beckoning welcome to the island.

But the visitor who sees Anglesey in its entirety is the air traveller. Flying in to one of the mainland airports on a fine day, he can admire a compact island. Much of its coastline of over 125 miles is a designated area of outstanding natural beauty. It is set in a sparkling sea.

To the traveller by sea from Ireland, the sight of the low-lying green fields of the north west coast stirs nostalgia, which gives way to eager anticipation as the steep cliffs of the North Stack mark the proximity of Holyhead harbour.

Whichever the approach, Anglesey is enticing. It is tourism orientated and there is plenty of information available about places of interest, leisure-time occupations, walks and outings, all to be had at the Tourist Information Centres.

But they do not tell the whole story. Extra knowledge of a location adds much richness to a visit, and the book sets out to offer this. I hope it also proves that many first impressions are worth a second look.

Crossing Traeth Lafan

Traeth Lafan on a calm, sunny day, presents a picture of peace. When the tide is out, there is a four-mile expanse of golden sand, warm and firm-looking. Thus, all the horror stories of crossings to Anglesey in bad weather in the days before the bridges seem inconceivable.

But if you know how treacherous weather and shifting sands can cause havoc, even in these days of sophisticated navigational aids, then you will understand those stories.

In days gone by, weary travellers to Anglesey from Abergwyngregyn had to walk out four miles to meet the ferry boat from Beaumaris. In poor weather those coming in the opposite direction, disembarking in mid channel with no moonlight to guide them, were guided by a tolling bell which sounded eerie in the blackness.

The Llanfaes ferry boat operated in the short time around low water, and the ferryman's job was probably a part-time one. He was given land near to where the ferry was tied, at what is now The Green, Beaumaris. He was therefore ready to take to the oars when necessary.

The ferry was in the charge of the Sheriff until the early 1300s, when it became the responsibility of the Constable of Beaumaris Castle.

Before the boat was transferred, it had an overhaul, and records still exist describing the work done and the cost. Ropes were bought. So were 11 oars at 2½d each; and 300 'nails of spiking' at 3d per 100. Iorwerth, the carpenter, and Madog, his assistant, worked for five days inserting new planks, using 'Roff' nails made by Roger the smith, who also repaired the anchor. Tallow and pitch were used to smear the boat. The Sheriff paid a total of 31s. 10½d, and the job was considered well done. But as the years passed, boats were often lost, and new ones built.

This was the main route to Holyhead and Ireland. It was used by civil servants, merchants, and travellers of all kinds, some of whom mentioned the ferry in their writings and diaries.

When Beaumaris became a post town, the ferry assumed even greater importance, although it was inconvenient and dangerous, and could only be used when the tide was right. During high water the post had to be taken through Bangor to the Porthaethwy ferry, and then back by land to Beaumaris to continue its journey across the island to Holyhead.

Although there are no plans or specifications to prove it, the boats must have been large. Troops were moved to and from Ireland in this way, as were horses and luggage. John Byng, the intrepid 18th century traveller and diarist, writing in 1784, said that one boat's cargo consisted of 30 people and 15 horses.

Charts from the 17th century show two ways across the sands. One from below Penmaenmawr on the mainland crossed more or less directly to Beaumaris. This was called the Low Water Way. The other began west of Penmaenmawr and curved its way to the same spot, where travellers would meet the ferry boat. Guide posts were fixed in the sand at intervals.

Later, Gallows Point, at the western entrance to Beaumaris, became the landing place for the ferry. William Bulkeley in his diary, writing on April 15, 1753, told the story of a Scotsman being drowned off Traeth Lafan because the ferryman refused, or neglected, to collect him.

> 'Two of the said ferrymen the morrow went in quest of the corpse, tore out his pockets and stole his money and afterwards finding his box and pack, carried them also away and hid them in the Point under gravel and tang, which some of the townspeople observing, four of them, two sailors and two shipwrights, went there in the night, took them up and shared them amongst them.'

The opening of the Suspension Bridge had the effect of by-passing Beaumaris. Travellers bowling their way in their carriages across this latest wonder of Wales, and along Thomas Telford's new road to Holyhead, must have been thankful that they did not have to subject themselves any longer to the vagaries of the weather, the tides, and the ferrymen to cross Traeth Lafan.

Directions:
Beaumaris is a mecca for tourists, having an Edwardian Castle, a gaol and courthouse among its attractions. For centuries it was Anglesey's capital town and principal port for travellers from the mainland, until the bridges were built. It is well signposted off the A5 road crossing the Britannia Bridge, from Menai Bridge town, and the A5025 from Amlwch.

Ynys Seiriol

Ynys Gorad Goch

In the Menai Strait, between the Britannia Bridge and Telford's Suspension Bridge, lies the largest of several islands, with a white-painted house perched comfortably above the high water mark. This is Ynys Gorad Goch. At low tide, two weirs can be seen clearly, one to the north and the other to the south of the little island.

Experts say that probably the earliest method of catching fish in any quantity was by stopping the mouths of narrow tidal creeks with brushwood or stones, through which the water would run off at ebb tide, leaving the fish inside the barrier, high and dry. When it was found that this barrier blocked the ingress of fish on the subsequent flood tide, some arrangement had to be made to allow them to pass the barrier while the tide was flowing. This could be an opening in the wall which would be closed at high water.

A similar method could be the building of a barrier across the channel between a small island and the mainland. The fish could pass around the outside of the island, to be carried towards the shore on the flood, but held by the barrier when trying to make their way through the channel on the ebb.

The angles of the weirs on Ynys Gorad Goch are so set to catch maximum quantities of fish passing through the Strait on the ebb tide.

There were several such weirs along the Strait, from Bangor to Caernarfon. The swift currents and the unusual combination of tides which meet near the Suspension Bridge created excellent conditions for this type of fishing.

These fisheries are very old. The earliest known document relating to Ynys Gorad Goch is dated 1590, when the island and its fishery was leased by the then Bishop of Bangor to a Thomas Fletcher of Treborth, for which he had to pay 'Three pounds and besides one Barell full of hearinges at the tyme of the hearing fishinge'.

A later map refers to this as 'Bishop's Island'. There is a Bishop's Room in part of the house which is an observation room, and above the centre window is a carving of a mitre, and below it, the inscription 'I.R.

Ynys Gorad Goch

1808'. This is a reference to John Randolph, Bishop of Bangor at the time. The story goes that Bishops would come to meditate here.

The island and fishing rights were eventually sold by the Ecclesiastical Commissioners in 1888, and from that time it has had a succession of private owners.

High tides can divide the island into two. On the smaller, easterly rock, stands a curing tower.

Tradition has it that Gorad Goch supplied fish, fresh or smoked herring, to several monasteries in Anglesey since the 13th century.

The fish traps caught bream, codling, dogfish, herring, garfish, gurnard, mackerel, plaice, pollack, salmon, sandeels, whitebait and whiting.

In the early years of the 20th century, it became fashionable for visitors to cross to the island to enjoy whitebait teas. They would walk down to the shore by a footpath through the Coed Môr woods, ring a bell placed on the shore for the purpose, and a boat would put out from the island to collect them. The Gorad Whitebait Tea consisted of a pot of tea, brown bread and butter, and whitebait 'fried in a basket', priced one shilling.

During very high tides in the spring and autumn, the water sometimes reaches the outside of the house on the front and west sides.

During one occupancy, in 1963, an attempt was made to plant a garden on the island, on the north and east side of the curing tower. It had previously been a dumping-ground for rubbish. It was divided into two separate areas, a rock garden and a herb garden. Because there was little soil, peat was added, and buckets of silt brought by the tide, and seaweed and compost. The gardeners had permission to collect leaf-mould from the Anglesey shore. After using silt, it was necessary to wait until the rain had washed away the salt before planting.

The gardeners found that dianthus, androsace, alyssum, campanula and cheiranthus all flourished. Helianthemums, mimulus, alpine phlox, primulas and polyanthus and saxifrage also did well. Needless to say, there were predators – snails, the wind, and terns were all a menace. But the herb garden produced a wonderful crop of parsley the first year.

Directions:

To see the island at close quarters from land, take the woodland path from the Britannia Bridge – Menai Bridge main road, to the east of the slip road. This leads down steeply to the shore, to the one-time landing place where the bell was hung to call the boat.

The Toll of the Bridge

Many Anglesey churches are to be found at the end of quiet lanes. No traffic passes. One visits on purpose. The local council ignores the by-ways, rarely sending the hedge trimmers or flail mowers to mangle the hedgerows, so wild plants are left in peace to grow willy-nilly, seed, and flourish again. The hedges present no safety hazard so they are left alone and are a joy to see at any time of the year.

The out-of-season holidaymaker, going for a walk down such a lane, can be rewarded. Early winter is the time of year when one appreciates the skeleton of a tree, and the colour and texture of its bark.

Standing still in a country lane, the silence is broken by all kinds of gentle sounds. The wind in the trees. Crisp golden leaves not yet blown from the hedges rustle like crumpled paper. Running water tinkling over tiny stones. A robin calls to his mate, brilliantly, urgently.

A slanting sun will light up an astonishing kaleidoscope of colour. Grey stone walls, mixed with the occasional slab of blue slate may be bare of summer green covering, but this is replaced by yellow-green moss and the green whorls of navelwort. Glossy green ivy covers the top of the walls, with pincushion black fruits standing up bravely against a thin wind. Gnarled ivy stems weave fantastic shapes above laneside grass flattened by recent heavy rain. Fresh green ferns stand to attention as though spring were only just around the corner, although some weeks might pass before new fronds uncurl.

The dainty Traveller's Joy – wild clematis – effervesces over a hawthorn hedge, its feathery plumes far more showy than the insignificant flowers they replace.

Tiny flowers still bloom bravely in the shelter of the hedge bottom – Herb Robert, freshly pink, and the exquisite minute yellow stars of a sedum. Haws hold promise of still more winter food for the birds, and rose hips shine brilliantly red in among a netting of thorned branches. Leaves, blown by recent gales, lie crisping along the laneside, their colours ranging from the green-yellow of the sycamore to the golden brown of oak.

These are delights for the visitor who is willing to leave the car and walk at leisure. One such lane leads down from the busy road close to the Britannia Bridge, signposted St Mary's Church.

But many people travel to Anglesey by rail every year, over Stephenson's Britannia Bridge. At one time the train thundered through great enclosed metal tubes, but since the disastrous fire in the 1970s the rail track is now open, and travellers have the added bonus of a spectacular view.

Down below the bridge on the Anglesey shore is the little parish church of St Mary's, Llanfairpwll. Here it is quiet. The sun glints on the rippling waters of the Strait, catching the swirling eddies where a vicious current races beneath the grey stone towers of the bridge.

The Caernarfonshire bank is dense with trees, right down to the water's edge, but the softer meadows of Anglesey are green and inviting. The only sound is the water lapping on the shore, and the cry of sea birds.

There is a simple monument on the edge of the church yard. It was built by the stonemasons of the Britannia Bridge in memory of 18 of their workmates. One epitaph reads . . .

> Sacred to the memory of
>
> WILLIAM BROOK of DEWSBURY, Yorkshire, who died of typhus fever on the 11th October 1847, in the 27th year of his age. He was principal accountant of Messrs. Nowell Hemingways and Pearson, contractor for the masonry of the Britannia bridge. He was universally respected and regarded, not only by his employers but by a large body of workmen engaged in the construction of the bridge and who erected this monument to his memory by voluntary subscription.

The dreaded typhus raged even in this beautiful corner of Wales. The Yorkshire contractors had to find 800 men to work on the scaffolding for the tubes, and on the stone towers which were to hold them. Many were recruited locally, but most of them were Yorkshiremen who left their homes and brought their families and their scant belongings to Caernarfonshire. Some lived in temporary shanties and hurriedly erected small wooden cottages. Others even gypsied in encampments. Sanitary conditions were primitive, and it is a safe guess that more must have suffered the same fate as white-collar worker William Brook, for typhus rarely struck singly.

A further 700 men were needed to build the iron tubes, and they and their families had to be accommodated in the shanties.

A wooden platform half a mile long, and covering an area of about three and a half acres, was built out into the water. On it were three large workshops to house the forges and the various machines for punching

Monument in the Churchyard, St Mary's Church, Llanfairpwll

and cutting plate iron, for hundreds of plates had to be riveted together.

It has been estimated that around two million rivets were used to build the massive tubes. There were five men to a riveting gang, two of whom were boys. One boy would snatch the white hot bolt from the forge, dash to the spot where his gang was working, and hurl the bolt 40 feet into the air to the other boy at the top of the square tube. He would pick it up with his pincers and race along to the riveters. One riverter's boy was said to be only ten years old. Could this have been the child the inscription on the monument records as 'William Howard, boy, died in 1848'?

Surely the most tragic death recorded on the monument is that of Emma, youngest daughter of James Greave of Lake Lock near Wakefield, who died at Britannia Bridge in 1849 when she was only five years old. We are not told her story, either, but perhaps she lived in one of the huts along the water's edge, where so many dangers could have befallen her. Those shanties and huts, the forges and wharves, have all disappeared. Nature has long since covered their traces.

The Britannia Bridge took a later toll. When the bridge was being rebuilt following the fire, three men died during its reconstruction, and their names are recorded on the memorial.

Directions:
Leave the Britannia Bridge with the first slip road in a westerly direction. The lane marked 'St Mary's Church' is almost immediately on the left.

Four Lions Fat

While walking down the lane to St Mary's Church, Llanfairpwll, past the entrance to Carreg Brân Hotel, a gated lane can be seen on the left below the railway bridge. High above, at the side of the railway track is one of the large stone lions, four of which guard the entrance and exit to the track across the Britannia Bridge. They were once prominent, but they are now partially hidden by the road deck.

The lions were designed and executed by John Thomas, a Gloucestershire orphan who went to work for his architect brother in Birmingham and learnt his trade there. Sir Charles Barry was so impressed by his sculpting that he engaged John Thomas to superintend the stone carving in the then new House of Commons. John Thomas was responsible for the statues on the north and south fronts; the panels bearing the arms of the kings and queens of England, from William the Conqueror to Queen Victoria; the statues and bosses for the Victoria Tower and the bosses in Saint Stephen's Hall.

Throughout John Thomas's comparatively short life of 49 years, he completed an enormous amount of work throughout the country. One of his proudest commissions was one from Prince Albert, who asked him to execute two large reliefs of Peace and War for Buckingham Palace.

The stone lions on the Britannia Bridge are each 25 ft. long and weigh 80 tons. They were made in 1848.

A rhyme which many local children learn is the one by Y Bardd Cocos:

Dau lew tew
Heb ddim blew
Dau'r ochr yma
A dau'r ochr drew.

Which can be translated as:

Four lions fat
Two ochr this
And two ochr that.
(Two this side, and two that side)

or the variant . . . Four fat lions
Without any hair;
Two over here
And two over there.

Lion on the Britannia Bridge

Back to School

When you pass any Anglesey infants' school these days, your eye will be arrested by colourful pictures done by young artists, covering the large windows. Spring flowers, Easter Eggs, Father Christmases, stars and snow, all in their seasons.

Reading the Log Books for Llanfairpwll British School, 1872-98, at the Archives Office in Llangefni, one cannot help but compare the lively attitude towards education today with the spartan, strict, and, it would seem, very unimaginative education received by Anglesey children a little over a century ago.

The British School at Llanfairpwll opened its doors on January 2nd, 1872, with 76 pupils. Its numbers fluctuated throughout the period covered by the Log Books between this figure and 100. Attendance was haphazard in the beginning, with plenty of comments such as 'few attended on account of the weather'.

Days off to attend special events were frequent – the Band of Hope meeting at Gaerwen was considered more important than lessons. There was no school on the day the foundation stone of the new chapel in the village was laid, and Sunday School trips always took precedence.

As in most country districts throughout Wales, child power on the farms was almost as important as manpower at certain times. Haymaking usually put paid to school activities, while the good weather held.

'The attendance was affected by the appearance of a group of mushrooms in the fields' commented the headmaster on one occasion. Another time, it was the harvesting of blackberries.

Tradition played a large part in country life. On December 17th, 1888, the headmaster wrote 'Christmas is approaching and the rich and wealthy distribute coals to the poor of the district. These two days are the worst yet for attendance.'

Lessons included arithmetic, dictation, reading, composition, singing and, for the girls, sewing. But the sewing mistress did not attend occasionally, when she was reported as 'busily engaged in preparing mourning for a family in the place for the occasion of a funeral'. First things first!

Bearing in mind the complaints of the teaching profession today, it is interesting to find similar complaints over a century ago. Lack of space in which to teach effectively, and, in particular, lack of materials. The arrival of a consignment of rulers and india rubbers received ecstatic welcome. The schoolmaster complained about bare walls, and announced with obvious delight the acquisition of a map of the world and some 'advertising pictures'.

There is frequent mention of truancy, and disinterest in lessons.

> 'Spent most of my time in the morning with Standard 1 finding them very careless with their sums – not taking enough trouble to make them neat and inclined to be inaccurate in the working of subtraction. A slight touch of the cane had the desired effect.'

Teachers came and went, and the school welcomed students from Bangor to help with lessons. Voluntary help was also welcomed.

This, and a lot more, in the Llanfairpwll British School Log Books paints a colourful picture of life in the village so many years ago.

Directions:
The Archives Office for Anglesey is on the first floor of the Council Office block on Glanhwfa Road, before reaching the town centre when approaching off the A5. Readers wishing to research manuscripts etc. not on the open shelves need a reader's card, which can be obtained at the Office on arrival. The collection includes many school Log Books. Telephone for information on opening hours – 01248 752080.

The Man Behind the Women's Institute

The grey corrugated iron hall by the side of the toll house in Llanfairpwll is always a focus of attention for coach parties as they pass through the village. The sign tells them that the Llanfairpwll Women's Institute was the first to be founded in Britain, in 1915. But what coach parties are rarely told – probably because the driver does not know – is that it was a man who encouraged the women of the village to form their group. So began a movement which continues to be an important force in the lives of many women throughout Britain today.

Agriculture at the turn of the century was changing. Small farmers were finding it more difficult to make ends meet, for a variety of reasons. It was with these problems in mind that co-operatives were formed and they, in turn, joined forces to form the Agricultural Organisations Society.

The position of women in society was changing, too. It was recognised that they had a role to play in country life. Their changing status had already been recognised in Canada, where the first Institute, an offshoot of the Farmers' Institute, had been formed at Stoney Creek in Ontario. The movement was gaining impetus in Canada.

Before the First World War, not much interest was shown in Britain. But four years of shortages, with women taking an increasingly important role in keeping life going at home, changed attitudes.

The man who was to be the local catalyst in the creation of the first Women's Institute in Britain was Colonel the Honourable R.S.G. Stapleton-Cotton, who was one of the foremost workers in the co-operative effort in agriculture in North Wales. He was the second son of Viscount Combermere, and had come to live at Plas Llwyn Onn on the estate of his nephew, the 4th Marquess of Anglesey.

The Colonel was a remarkable man, who had lived an adventurous life. He served in South Africa as a second lieutenant in the Zulu War. While under canvas, his tent was struck by lightning during a violent thunderstorm, and he was paralysed in both legs from the knees down. On leaving the army, he became Inspector General of Police in British Guyana for a short time, then, on retirement in middle age, came to Anglesey.

Although crippled, his energy was unbounded. He provided a boost to the local economy by establishing a bacon factory, an egg-collecting depot, a chicory farm and a bulb farm in and around Llanfairpwll. He drained the marsh in the centre of the village by planting willow trees. He served on several agricultural committees, was a member of the University College Council in Bangor, served on military tribunals, and had a special interest in the rush mat industry at Newborough.

He was an enthusiastic and knowledgeable gardener, and wrote a practical guide to gardening, aimed at the small-holder and cottager. And he was a practised knitter, whose garments were much sought after among local society ladies! All these activities were conducted from his wheelchair.

The Agricultural Organisations Society was to meet in the University at Bangor in 1915. Mrs Watt, one of the W.I. organisers from Canada, was invited to speak on the role of women in country matters. Immediately following this meeting Col. Stapleton-Cotton called the women of Llanfairpwll together in the village, and Mrs Watts spoke to them. At that meeting, the W.I. in Britain was born. The first President was the Colonel's wife.

Such was the esteem in which the Colonel was held, the Llanfairpwll W.I. made him a member, and he – and his dog, Tinker – paid their subscriptions yearly until the Colonel, following his wife's death in 1924, decided to emigrate to live in St John's, Antigua, where he had a sugar plantation.

Before leaving, he had a leg amputated, and reported that for the first time in twenty years he was free from pain.

On his departure, Colonel Stapleton-Cotton's many friends in North Wales gave him a parting gift of a motor car, with the message: 'We hope it will help you in your many activities in your new home, and at the same time remind you of your friends in North Wales whose warm wishes go with you.'

The bacon factory, the egg-packing depot and the market garden have long since disappeared. But the name of Colonel Stapleton-Cotton is well remembered in Llanfairpwll. He was a big man, with a big heart.

Directions:

The W.I. Hall stands next to the Llanfairpwll toll house, at the entrance to the village when approaching from the Britannia Bridge. The bacon factory and egg-packing depot were alongside the railway and they have disappeared. Plas Llwyn Onn is in private hands. It stands in trees, back off the A4080, between Plas Newydd and Brynsiencyn. The market garden was in the fields on the opposite side of the road.

Where Rhododendrons Reign Supreme

The gardens at Plas Newydd, home of the 7th Marquess of Anglesey and now in the hands of the National Trust, are a joy in every season.

In early spring great sweeps of daffodils and other narcissi nod in the breeze on the smooth lawns sloping down to the house and the shore. Tall trees show early promise, tipped with fresh green. A few weeks later, azaleas and waxen magnolias vie for notice south of the house, and with the lengthening days and warmer air, they are followed by banks of rhododendrons in all their glory in the special garden north of the house. Come midsummer, and the terrace garden is splashed blue, reflecting the colour of the sparkling Strait as agapanthus stand sentinel.

As summer flowers fade, autumn tints appear as the creeper covering the south of the house turns russet red.

The view across the Strait from the house cannot have changed much since the time when the first Marquess commissioned Humphrey Repton to landscape the grounds at Plas Newydd. Repton, a landscape gardener, admired the work of his predecessor, 'Capability' Brown, but produced his own scaled down ideas to meet the needs of the lesser estates. He did not work on such a grand scale as his mentor.

Repton would visit a client, walk and measure the land, and offer his suggestions for development in what were termed 'Red Books', so called because they were all bound similarly in red. He sketched before-and-after drawings of the garden, sometimes adding cut-outs pasted over the drawings to show several possibilities. These were accompanied by a written description, leaving the client in no doubt about the method of working and the result.

The Red Book for Plas Newydd still exists. It shows extensive tree planting and landscaping. After Repton's death in 1818, his ideas were extended by the 1st Marquess of Anglesey.

Blue Atlas cedars, tulip and maidenhair trees add interest. In the early years of this century the 6th Marquess developed the woodland still further, especially to the south of the house in the area known as 'The West Indies' – a name which no-one today, even in the family, can explain. Decidious azaleas, camellias, Japanese maples and magnolias have matured, and are now splendidly colourful features of this part of the garden. Camellias were transplanted from the greenhouses at Beaudesert in Staffordshire, the former family seat now demolished.

This part of the garden was abandoned during the Second World War. It is thanks to the initiative and enthusiasm of the present Marquess, and his own additional planting during the 1950s and 1960s, that it now appears so attractive.

Extensive hedges of viburnum, Chilean Firebush and hydrangeas add to the attraction.

There was once a conservatory north of the house, but this was demolished, and an Italianate garden designed on its foundations. This is a picture in summer with its water cascade, the latest addition, splashing among the stones, and the deep borders a mass of blue agapanthus.

But the chief feature of the garden at Plas Newydd is undoubtedly the Rhodondendron Garden. Planting began here in the 1930s when the 6th Marquess took advantage of mature trees in the Grand Lodge Wood, which afforded a wind and weather brake to shelter young saplings

The Second World War intervened, and the garden was abandoned. It was left to the present Marquess to take on the awesome task of clearing and rescuing the species which had not succumbed to neglect in order to continue the project. The late Lord Aberconway made the Marquess and Marchioness a unique wedding present of a great number of thinnings from his own famous garden at Bodnant in the Conwy Valley, along with the labour to transplant them at Plas Newydd. Among these were hybrids which make the main body of the important collection today. Since then, other scented species and hybrids have been added, along with magnolias and eucryphias.

A walk in the Rhododendron Garden in season is an experience not to be missed, especially now that a path has been cleared along the water's edge, making the approach even more delightful. A notice in the entrance hall of the house tells the visitor what is flowering at any particular time.

Plas Newydd Gardens are now in the hands of the National Trust, but the 7th Marquess still maintains a 'hands-on' interest in their development and upkeep.

Directions:
Plas Newydd is one mile south-west of Llanfairpwll and the A5, on the A4080 to Brynsiencyn; turn off the road from the Britannia Bridge by the Llanfairpwll tollhouse, and follow the National Trust sign.

Rhododendron

The Treasure of Llyn Cerrig Bach

To the south east of Llanfair-yn-neubwll, on the road skirting the edge of R.A.F. Valley, close to the public viewing area, is a series of small lakes and pools where the land is a marsh.

One of these lakes, Llyn Cerrig Bach, was found to contain a splendid collection of late Iron Age metalwork and animal bone. This came to light during the Second World War. During the winter of 1942/3, peat was extracted from around the lake edge, to be used for consolidating the sand dunes (Tywyn Trewan) on which the runways at the station were built. Wind-blown sand from the dunes had been causing damage to the aircraft engines.

Peat was extracted mechanically, spread across the sandy area of the airfield, then sown with grass seed to stabilise the dunes. While local workmen were moving the peat, they began to discover iron and bronze objects mixed with animal bones.

Now some 140 objects from the site are in the safe hands of the National Museum of Wales in Cardiff. They represent one of the most important collections of Iron Age material in the British Isles. It is thought by archaeologists and historians that Llyn Cerrig Bach must have been a sacred offering place, into which loot was thrown as a gift to the gods. The collection includes spears, daggers, plaques, bridle-bits, gang chains, harness, shield bosses and decorative bronze-work.

Experts have studied these objects using modern scientific equipment and techniques, including metallurgical analysis and radio carbon-dating.

One fact which has come to light since the initial discovery is that not all the objects dug up were collected by the archaeologists. Before their significance was realised, several pieces were taken home by men working at the airfield. Over the years, many of the owners of the pieces allowed them to be studied, but it is believed that unrecorded objects may remain in private hands, and more may still be buried beneath the surface, sealed under the runway.

The Anglesey Antiquarian Society and Field Club has erected a stone on the site of the find, which can be read from the road.

Directions:

From the south, leave the A5 by turning left at the R.A.F. Valley sign (cross-roads with the road to Bodedern) and proceed to the small lakes, through Llanfihangel-yn-Nhywyn. The drive can then be continued through Llanfair-yn-neubwll to return to the A5 at Caergeiliog.

Mona Green Marble

Small quarries abound in Anglesey, their products reflecting the variety of stone available on the island. Between Bodior and Four Mile Bridge; and at Mynachdy, Llanfair-yng-Nghornwy, are two quarries which have supplied unusual stone, examples of which have been much sought after in recent years – Mona Green Marble.

Angharad Llwyd the Anglesey historian, in her prize-winning essay at the Beaumaris Eisteddfod of 1832, referred to the green marble quarries 'which first came into the notice of the late Mr Bullock who manufactured a magnificent table of green marble which was sent to Buonaparte at St Helena.' This table was part of the furnishings of the 56-room bungalow which the British government built for its eminent prisoner.

Travellers to Anglesey over the years have noted the serpentine marble. Fenton, in 1810, referred to these quarries 'lately discovered'; Pennant, forty years earlier, described the marble as 'green, black and a dull purple'. Llanfechell and the Skerries were also mentioned as sources for the stone.

A recent article in a national newspaper described George Bullock as 'a furniture maker of the calibre of Chippendale'. It is believed he gained control of the quarries in Anglesey, which he promoted under the name of Mona Marble, in 1806. He was a natural artist and designer, and originally a wax modeller whose mother ran a waxworks museum in Birmingham. The family moved to Liverpool, where he began his career in cabinet making and general furnishing, and where he founded the Liverpool Academy.

In Great Tew Park in Oxfordshire, a despatch box containing his bills and correspondences about the furnishing of that mansion has been discovered. Bullock supplied furniture for Sir Walter Scott's home at Abbotsford, and made a suite of furniture for the Duke of Palmella, the Portuguese Ambassador to Britain, which was sold in 1987 for £220,000.

Angharad Llwyd visited Trentham, where the owner, the Duke of Sutherland, showed her 'a beautiful chimney piece made of Mona marble'. He told her that it compared favourably with the 'verd antique' which he had imported from Rome. At Plas Rhianfa, the large house at

Glyn Garth, on the road from Menai Bridge to Beaumaris, there are chimney pieces with panels of green marble brought by Sir John Hay Williams from his farm at Cruglas, Valley, not far from the local quarry.

George Bullock died in 1818, aged 35, which would make him only 23 years old when he acquired the quarries in Anglesey.

Directions:

To find the quarry, now partly covered with vegetation, take the narrow road marked Rhoscolyn shortly after crossing the Inland Sea at Four Mile Bridge from the direction of Valley.

To Tyger – In Memoriam

The sea has always played a large part in the story of Anglesey. It can be cruel, as is reflected in the story of Tyger.

Near the edge of the cliffs between Rhoscolyn and Trearddur Bay stands a memorial stone, two feet high. On the seaward face is the inscription 'Tyger, September 17th, 1819'. This commemorates a dog's unselfish devotion in saving the lives of a captain, two men and a boy after their ship had foundered on the rocks.

The story goes that a ketch, bound for Liverpool, struck Maen Piscar, a dangerous rock some three quarters of a mile offshore, during a thick fog which had lasted several days. Lifted by a swell, she slipped off the rock and after drifting for a short while before an onshore wind, sank in deep water.

As the vessel sank, the captain's retriever, Tyger, leaped into the sea and began to swim. His master, realising that their only chance of life lay in trusting to the dog's instinct, struck out in pursuit, calling to the others to do the same. The captain was a strong swimmer. The boy hung on to Tyger's collar and after a long struggle they sighted the cliffs looming through the fog.

But for the gallant behaviour of the dog, it is doubtful whether any of them would have reached land, as they were exhausted. Tyger, having brought the boy within reach of the rocks, turned and swam back to his master. The captain, although exhausted himself, saw that one of the men was struggling and sent Tyger back to him. The dog seized the man by the collar and helped him to land. He turned to help his master and the other sailor, and eventually they all lay on the shore, completely exhausted.

The captain, the two men and the boy recovered. But Tyger feebly licked his master's hand and died. The stone stands above where the final tragedy happened.

Directions:
The memorial stands on the coastal path, opposite Maen Piscar, between Rhoscolyn and Trearddur Bay.

Waiting to Sail

Seeing the handsome new ferry-rail terminal at Holyhead, and the busy traffic which goes through the port, especially in the summer, the way to Ireland appears to have been made very easy. But the weather still has the final word, and even the latest ship in the fleet still has to stay in port if the treacherous Irish Sea is in a particularly bad mood.

However, things are certainly better than they were when Dean Swift, author of 'Gulliver's Travels', was delayed in 1727.

> 'September 26: Thoughts upon being confined at Holyhead . . . as a passenger who is in a scurvy, unprovided, comfortless place without one companion and who therefore wants to be at home, where he hath all conveniences there proper for a gentleman of quality. Here at Holyhead I cannot read at night and I have no books to read in the day. I have no subject in my head at present to write on. I dare not send my linen to be washed for fear of being called away to sail at half an hour's warning, and then I must leave them behind me, which is a serious point. In the meantime, I am in danger of being lousy, which is a ticklish point.
>
> I live at great expense without one comfortable bite or sup. I am afraid of joyning with passengers for fear of getting acquaintance with the Irish. The days are short and I have five hours at night to spend by myself before I go to bed. I should be glad to converse with farmers or shopkeepers, but none of them speak English. A dog is better company than the Vicar, for I remember him of old. What can I do but write everything that comes into my head . . . I confine myself to my narrow chamber in all unwalkable hours. The master of the pacquet-boat, one Jones, hath not treated me with the least civility . . . In short, I come from being used as an Emperor (in London) to being used worse than a dog at Holyhead.'

The diarist, William Bulkeley of Brynddu, Llanfechell, was no stranger to the vagaries of the weather in the Irish Sea. He often travelled to Ireland where he would stay with his cousin, visit the theatre, do some necessary shopping, looked to his estates there, visited the cattle market and went to church. He explains how miserable the crossing could be.

> 'Sailing against the wind, we would make very little way in rough seas. I mind one such voyage, when we weighed anchor at four in the morning for our return journey to Holyhead, but the wind being strong and due east we stretched the six hours' ebb to the north and the six hours' flood to the south to gain only two leagues in a tide. Before night, we were got within four or five leagues of the Head, but about sunset a great storm arose and blew easterly all the night, and by the morning we were drove back again in sight of the Irish shore, and had to turn back to Dublin. It was not until several days later that the weather allowed us a safe passage to Holyhead.'

Traffic to and from the Irish capital prompted Lewis Morris, an Anglesey man well versed in the seas around the coast, in a letter to the secretary of the Admiralty in 1748, to urge improvements to the harbour. As it happened, his suggestions were implemented, but not until long after he had died.

He wrote –

> 'This is also found to be a very convenient Harbour for the Northern trade, when taken short by contrary winds, but as it is only one of rough draughts of Nature, which showed what ought to be done (and Men never gave it a helping hand), it is on N.W. winds no good lying-place for large shipping.
>
> If this Harbour was repaired, and warehouses built here, it would be a very convenient Place for the Irish to import their Goods that pay English duty . . . and the Dublin Merchants might have the Conveniency, by the packet-boats, of going over to see their Goods landed. A pier might be run out to the S.E. from the Salt House, on the south point of Salt Island, within which large vessels might lie afloate; also the North Sound, and the Sound of Parry's Island, ought to be walled up, which would prevent the Swell in the Harbour. This may be done with the Expence of between Four and Five thousand pounds.'

A breakwater was built at Holyhead between 1845 and 1873. This proved to be a massive task. One and a half miles long, it snaked out to sea from the north-west of the town, with another pier from Salt Island. These partially enclose a large stretch of water which shelters many ships in stormy weather.

Directions:

To the breakwater, enter Holyhead on the A5 and where the road forks, bear right alongside the railway in the direction of Salt Island. Turn left at the end of the A5 along Beach Road to keep to the sea, passing the coastguard station, towards Porth-y-felin. Then along a promenade to Soldier's Point and the beginning of the breakwater.

Brynddu, Llanfechell

Four Months of Hell

A visit to the Maritime Museum on the water's edge at Holyhead recalls the sea-faring life of the port over the years. No story is more heart-rending than that of the fate of H.M.S. 'Tara' and its crew, during the early years of the First World War.

Immediately before the war, sea crossings from Holyhead to Dublin were operated by the London & North Western Railway Company. On the outbreak of war, one of those ships, 'Hibernia', was requisitioned by the Admiralty, given armaments and re-fitted for patrol service. 'Hibernia' was re-named 'Tara'.

Between 1914 and the late summer of 1915, she saw service in the narrow waters between Scotland and Ireland. She later received orders to sail to the Mediterranean to become part of the North Egyptian coastal patrol.

On Friday, November the 5th, 1915, 'Tara' was sighted by a German submarine, eight miles off Solum on the North African coast, and torpedoed. Ninety-three of the crew scrambled to the boats before she sank within eight minutes. The boats were taken in tow by the submarine, and landed at Port Suliman. The crew was handed over to Turkish officers based there, to begin what was to be a cruel experience in the Libyan desert.

The prisoners were moved constantly, being made to march miles in a day, 'up and down mountains, most of the crew with bare feet, roads in awful condition, slept in old rock caves' wrote one crew member in his diary.

On their first day they buried the cook on the shore, covering his grave with a mound of stones to prevent any disturbance by wolves or native dogs.

William Thomas had returned to the sinking ship to try to save a fellow seaman, and when he finally reached the lifeboat his leg was crushed between it and the side of 'Tara', resulting in a compound fracture. He spent several days in agony, with no medical attention, and was forced to march with the others, the guards using their rifle butts to urge him on. Eventually septicaemia set in and the Turkish doctor attached to the camp was forced to operate, without anaesthetic or proper instruments, to remove his leg. This he did with a sharp stone and blunt scissors.

Paymaster Alfred Dutton, in his diary, records William's death.

> '14th November, William Thomas died 11.30 p.m. the previous night. Buried at 8.30 a.m. Very touching service was held by Captain Tanner, nearly everyone crying. Most pathetic scene. Hymns sung in evening by whole crew. Everyone feeling very lonely and quiet.'

During the next weeks, their plight deteriorated. Food became scarce, and they lived on a sparse diet of boiled rice, green tea, boiled goat or sheep. Towards the end of their imprisonment, white snails were gathered by the bucketful and boiled to supplement the menu. On the few occasions when flour was issued, ingenuity came into play. By now, the crew had been divided into messes, each mess cooking its own rations. There were nine officers in Alfred Dutton's mess.

> '16th December (42nd day): Breakfast at 7.30, hard boiled rice. Having had a little more flour issued to us in lieu of shortness of rice, I managed to knead some flour and boiled rice together and wrapped some in a leg of a Mahomed trousers and boiled it in a bucket. This proved a great success, nice and plump. It was divided into nine pieces and each with a big chunk in his hand and some tea in glasses, had a fine dinner. We promised another one for ourselves at Christmas.'

As was inevitable, dysentery was rife. On the 22nd of December, Dutton recorded:

> 'Breakfast we had one beaker of rice boiled in Olive Oil which had been given to us the previous night on account of terrible dysentery in camp. Late in day working party returned from well and had a deputation for more food, without success. Simply cruel working men on such a diet. One small goat killed. Meat kept for a future date. All terribly hungry.'

They made snail soup, and when a few dates were offered they even used the stones, ground finely, to provide ersatz coffee.

The guards were also facing starvation. By March 1916 the situation was such that Dutton wrote

'Three sheep are killed, all inside parts of two are being taken away, also two heads, by the guards. Firewood party all feeling really done up.

Can hardly walk – on our knees taking the wood, no energy left to pull some up by the roots. Dinner and tea, boiled rice. Today looks very serious and very little hopes. Myself I don't feel like walking four yards but struggle on. Managed to gather more wood and more green vegetation and garlic. Dinner, boiled mutton and soup. Feeling done up. Must go for a good sleep. All officers and men are breaking down, some fainting in heat.'

This was Paymaster Dutton's last entry. While writing, he was not to know that freedom was approaching. The next day the camp was relieved unexpectedly by a convoy of motor vehicles led by the Duke of Westminster, which included several ambulances.

One can imagine the incredulity and delight which the approaching convoy must have created among these emaciated men. They had suffered so severely for almost five months, with no knowledge of what was going on beyond the desert.

Paymaster Dutton, along with the other 'Tara' survivors, was taken to Alexandria to recuperate in hospital before returning home to a heroes' welcome in Holyhead. The maritime museum has pictures showing the men at a home-coming celebration.

Directions:
The Maritime Museum is on Beach Road, Holyhead on the New Harbour shore.

From Chapel of Rest to School

The small building near the south gate to St Cybi's church in Holyhead is all that remains of the nave of a previous church on the site. Called 'Capel y Bedd', it is now used as a Church Room. The building has seen several uses since it was erected, one being a school first opened over 250 years ago thanks to the then rector, the Reverend Thomas Ellis.

A Holyhead historian, Lucy Williams, spoke affectionately of this hard-working cleric when she told his story to the Anglesey Antiquarian Society at a lecture in 1947. Thomas Ellis had, in his own words, 'real concern for ye swarm of children, which grow in a manner wild for want of schooling' and which, he hoped, 'will thro' the Chancellor's means (Chancellor Wynne, brother to an influential parishioner) be put in a way of serving God and man.'

Thomas Ellis's letters survive. Through them, we can feel the urgency of his submissions to reconstruct 'Capel y Bedd' as a free school for the poor children of Holyhead. He was a persistent correspondent, often apologetic for his enthusiasm ' . . . fears the Chancellor thinks me troublesome and is offended at my frequent applications.' Nevertheless, the project was 'always uppermost in my head and heart.' His pleas were noted, and eventually the money was forthcoming. The chapel was adapted, and the builders' bills can be seen at the National Library of Wales.

As with many letter-writers of his day, Thomas Ellis's character shines through the words he penned. He kept in touch with Hugh Owen of Penrhos, Holyhead's stately home at the time, who was an invalid at Bristol Spa. His letters must have been a lifeline between Hugh and his family in Holyhead, especially during the birth of Hugh's daughter, Margaret, which happened in his absence and whom he was never to see. The description of the christening and the 'little Miss – as pretty a young lady as ever one would desire to toast' and her mother, 'as brave and jolly' must have brought tears to the eyes of the sick father. Such was Thomas Ellis.

Thomas Ellis's school, as it came to be known, remained at 'Capel y Bedd' until 1817, when the two-storey National School was built

Capel y Bedd

elsewhere in the town. The original building reverted to church use.

The present school continues to carry the name of its founder.

Directions:
St Cybi's church stands high above the harbour. The approach is along the main shopping street.

A Sailor Remembered

One of the outstanding features of Holyhead, which greets the visitor arriving from Ireland, is the tall obelisk on the Alltran Rock, high above the harbour. Perched over 80 feet above high water, this is a suitable site to place a memorial to a man who played an important role in the maritime history of the port.

John Macgregor Skinner was American by birth, born around 1760, the son of the King's Attorney General for New Jersey. Because his father sided with the royal cause during the War of Independence, the family was banished from the mainland. Their estates were sequestered, and they lived the remainder of their time in America on Long Island.

John Macgregor Skinner saw many years' service at sea, in a variety of situations. Margaret Owen of Penrhos, Holyhead, wrote a letter to her grandson at St John's College, Cambridge in 1800, saying 'a gentleman, Captain Skinner, who has but one arm . . . a very pleasant agreeable Gentleman. He lost his arm in the American War when a boy but 11 years old, can shuffle and deal the cards with his left hand much better than I can, and is most aggreeable affable, he is very cheerful and is always the same in company.' In 1780 he saw action and received a head wound which resulted in the loss of his right eye.

After his naval service came to an end, Skinner joined the Post Office department, and in the late 1790s was appointed to command the 'Princess Augusta', one of the packet boats used to convey foreign mails from Falmouth. Later came command of the 'Princess Royal' on the same service.

The duty of the Foreign Mail Packet Service included defence of the mail which, at times, could be a dangerous operation. One such action took place off the Western Isles as the ship carried American mail. His ship, which had only six guns, was chased by a well-manned French brig, with which Skinner kept up a running fight of several hours. Eventually, the French ship moved away and Skinner's ship sailed on. One of Captain Skinner's sisters, and a female servant, her two daughters, who were returning to America, were so inspired by the gallantry of their defenders that they worked in the magazine, filling cartridges and also assisting the surgeon.

On his return to England, the Postmaster General presented Captain Skinner with 50 guineas, and a similar sum to be distributed among the crew.

Skinner's association with Holyhead began in 1799, when he was appointed to command the 'Leicester', a packet boat sailing between Holyhead and Dublin. This marked the beginning of 32 years during which he made the town his home and made frequent sailings between Anglesey and Ireland.

John Macgregor Skinner was liked universally. As well as Margaret Owen, who commented on his character, a writer of the times said of him: 'He was praised for his bland and urbane manners towards all classes passing to and from Ireland, and also a zealous discharge of his duty . . . His hospitality was unbounded and open-hearted.' The poor of Holyhead regarded him as a kind and generous friend.

Skinner's ship was chosen to convey the Lords Lieutenant of Ireland, and he was honoured by George IV who commanded him to convey the royal party to Howth. The king wished to bestow a knighthood on him, but Skinner refused the honour. He was instead promoted to the rank of Commander, presented with a gold snuff box, and his packet was re-named 'Royal Sovereign George IV'.

Land-based sports interested him. He was especially keen on hunting, supported the local harriers, and he owned horses. He was equally popular on the other side of the Irish Sea and this was demonstrated in 1804 when, after losing his ship in a storm which battered it on loose stones surrounding the base of the lighthouse in Dublin Bay, the merchants of Dublin raised enough money to buy a new packet boat which was presented to him.

Captain Skinner was outspoken in his criticism of the management of the Post Office. The ships were so badly constructed, he said, that they could not be compared to those he had commanded earlier. His ship by now was the 'Escape', about which he was most dissatisfied, complaining that the bulwarks needed strengthening. This complaint was made to the House of Commons.

He also complained that high fares and poor accommodation for passengers were losing Holyhead trade, with passengers preferring the more up to date vessels and better conditions of the Liverpool service, although the sea journey was much longer.

On October the 30th, 1832, 'Escape', ironically named as it happened, was returning to Holyhead from Howth when, about a mile and a half

Skinner Monument, Holyhead

from Holyhead pier, the sea struck the starboard quarter and burst into the bulwark where Captain Skinner and his mate were standing. The force of the water swept them across the deck, taking the binnacle with them, and forcing them through the lee bulwark into the sea.

A few days later the body of Captain Skinner, fully dressed, was sighted in the water floating towards the South Stack. Efforts to retrieve it were hampered as the weather took a turn for the worse.

Conditions improved during the day, and his body was sighted near the rocks on the Penrhosfeilw shore, floating in the opposite direction, and impossible to retrieve. The following day, Skinner's corpse floated ashore in Porthdafarch bay, by this time headless and naked. This gave cause for much conjecture. Some believed that his body had been robbed and then sunk with a weight from which, when it became buoyant by fermentation, it released itself and floated to the shore, leaving the head behind.

John Macgregor Skinner's remains were buried in the lower churchyard at Holyhead. He was a sailor of 72 years of age, who had served his country and the town of Holyhead well. He is remembered further by a marble tablet on the south side of the chancel in the parish church.

The inscription on the obelisk above the harbour reads

> 'This monument was erected by his numerous friends to the memory of John Macgregor Skinner, R.M. and for 33 years Captain of one of the Post Office packets on this station, in testimony of his virtues and their affectionate remembrance of him in his public capacity. He was distinguished for zeal, intrepidity and fidelity. In private life he was a model of unvarying friendship, disinterested kindness and unbounded charity. MDCCCXXXII.

Directions:
The Skinner Monument stands above the harbour at Morawelon. There is no public access to it, but it can be seen at close quarters from the estate of houses surrounding it on three sides. It can be reached by taking the first turn left out of Holyhead on the A5 after crossing the railway bridge, and climbing the hill.

A Welsh grave for a Royal Yacht

The treacherous, rocky coast of Anglesey has seen many ships wrecked as they attempted to round Carmel Head in bad weather, passing between the mainland and the small group of islands the Vikings christened The Skerries.

A lighthouse was set up on the largest island in 1716, using a coal fire in a brazier. The then owners were allowed to levy a charge to ships, and they became very wealthy on the proceeds. Since 1841, this has been a Trinity House lighthouse. It is now, like that at South Stack, fully automated.

The Welsh name, Ynysoedd y Moelrhoniaid, denotes its popularity with seals, and many sea-birds nest there.

Of the wrecks, none was so famous as that of the 'Mary', the first royal yacht.

When Charles, Pretender to the English throne, was banished to the continent in the 17th century, he spent time in Holland where his sister, Mary, had married William, the Prince of Orange. When Charles was proclaimed King of England, William was determined that he should arrive for his coronation with suitable pomp, and provided one of the Dutch royal yachts to take him on the first lap of his journey to London.

Charles was entranced with the yacht, so the Prince of Orange ordered that a similar ship, then being built for the Dutch East India Company, be bought and presented to him for his use on the River Thames.

Britain's first royal yacht was named the 'Mary' in honour of the king's sister, and no expense was spared on her fittings and decor. A contemporary account gives a detailed description, mentioning her sprit mainsail and staysail, and her nine bronze guns. 'Mary' was manned by a crew of thirty. She was 52ft long, 19ft wide and 7ft 7 inches deep. Her burthen was 100 tonnes.

The diarist, Samuel Pepys, wrote in his diary in November 1660 after being invited on board: 'the yacht is indeed one of the finest things that I ever saw for neatness and room in so small a vessel.'

However, 'Mary's' life as a royal yacht was short. She was found to be unsuited to conditions in the Thames, and eventually Commissioner Pett of the Royal Navy was instructed to build a larger vessel with a deeper draught. So 'Mary' disappeared from the Thames, and was put into service with the Royal Navy to carry important passengers between Ireland and England.

While on one such trip in March 1675, the weather being foggy and visibility bad, 'Mary' was wrecked in forty feet of water close to the Skerries, and began to sink. There was little time for rescue, but as she capsized, her unusually long mainmast touched the rocks and thirty-nine of the passengers and crew were able to reach the shore. The captain, the bo'sun, the Earl of Meath and thirty-three other passengers were lost.

This took place before any light was put on the Skerries, and the north coast of Anglesey was then wild and sparsely populated. It was some time before the survivors were rescued, but they managed to keep alive by making a fire from jetsam, and regaling themselves with wine from a cask which had drifted ashore.

No attempt was made to salvage anything from the 'Mary' until a chance happening in 1971, when members of two separate Lancashire sub aqua clubs were diving in the vicinity on the same day, looking for lobsters. Instead of lobsters, they found two of 'Mary's' bronze guns, and immediately interest in the wreck was sparked.

Marine researchers were alerted, mainly at the University of Liverpool, who persuaded the rival groups to work together to provide a pre-disturbance survey. This was undertaken quickly, as the Protection of Wrecks Act was not yet in force and it was feared that vandals might dive to loot.

Conserving the main items – the nine bronze guns – proved to be a problem. According to law, the guns had to remain in the hands of the Local Receiver for twelve months at least, so they were stored in a bicycle shed until room could be made for them in safer quarters.

At the time, Liverpool Museum was undergoing great changes, and was hard pressed to accommodate more artefacts of any kind. But the then curator used his ingenuity and saw to the construction of deep vats, made from heavy timbers, lined with polythene, and filled with water which was changed regularly. These housed the guns, so that they would not disintegrate through exposure to the air, until they could be treated.

The Maritime Museum at Liverpool now cares for nearly 1500 objects from the site. They included the nine guns, nearly 300 silver coins, 'Mary's' anchor, and numerous pieces of fine tableware and jewellery which probably belonged to the captain or the more wealthy passengers.

All the objects, including parts of a skeleton of a young woman passenger, have been systematically examined, recorded and

Skerries Lighthouse

photographed. There is a small display in the third floor gallery of the museum.

Directions:
There are glimpses of the Skerries from various points along the A5025, but more clearly from the village of Llanfair-yng-Nghornwy (signposted off the A5025 between Llanrhuddlad and Tregele), and from Carmel Head where there is a footpath from the village, or from Mynachdy.

Amlwch – Town with a Past

Visitors to Amlwch should travel a little farther, and look for Amlwch Port to appreciate the atmosphere of Amlwch in days gone by.

The little town grew in importance speedily with the development of the copper industry at Mynydd Parys. In the first half of the 18th century it was a mere hamlet. Then things changed and Bingley, writing after touring Wales, explained Amlwch was 'entirely dependent for its prosperity on the copper mines for most of its inhabitants have some concern in them, either as miners or agents'.

As the town grew, so did the importance of its port. Nicholas Owen Junior of Llandyfrydog, in his 'History of Anglesey' writes

> 'Amlwch harbour in the north west part of Anglesey is a small cove, formed as it were by an excavation of a large rock, the extension of which, as far as navigable, we compute without measurement to be 40 perches. When the tide is in, tis here nothing strange to see men fishing while they stand on the brim of the excavation; in this agreeable pastime they avoid those commotions often concomitants of sea fishing. The harbour is much frequented by small sloops; herewith Liverpool pilot boats usually moor, to be ready to give assistance to such vessels as are unacquainted with the coast. The village of Amlwch is seated near half a mile off the shore. It has a considerable market on Friday and a fair for cattle on November 11th.'

The harbour became a bustling place, where not only copper ore was shipped, but there was brisk trade from vessels known as 'flats', bringing in barm bought by the local brewery from Thomas Greenall of the celebrated family of Lancashire brewers. At the end of the 18th century, the little town of Amlwch had over sixty ale houses.

In spite of its industrialisation, Amlwch still appealed to the writer Thomas Aikin as a tourist attraction. He painted a pleasant picture when he wrote

> 'As we approached Amlwch we were much pleased with seeing the scars of rock between the town and the sea occupied by numerous

groups of men, women and children, all most neat in their best clothes, it being Sunday, who were enjoying the mild temperature of a summer evening, rendered refreshed by the neighbourhood of the sea . . . I am acquainted with no place the manner of whose inhabitants are so unexceptional as Amlwch . . . not a single substance have I known of drunkenness, not one quarrel have I witnessed during two very crowded market days . . . and I believe no gaol or bridewell or house of confinement exists in the town or neighbourhood. The town of Amlwch which about 30 years ago had no more than half a dozen houses in the whole parish now supports a population of four or five thousand.'

But not everyone shared Aikin's views.

James Treweek, the mine agent, said 'Amlwch is one of the worst places I ever knew for young men to be brought up in . . . because of the many pot houses in the town and the company who attend them regularly.'

In the Mona Mine manuscripts, there is a comment on the town's medical profession . . . 'There are three doctors at Amlwch. One is a drunkard, the second lacks experience and surgical skill, and the third is habitually in the same condition as the first.'

Bearing these comments in mind, it is not surprising that Robert Roberts, the Amlwch schoolmaster in those days, was glad to leave.

'I left Amlwch with a sigh of relief, shaking its black dust from off my feet and leaving its smoky atmosphere as one might leave the close air of a prison, to live in Ruthin where I might reasonably expect to live among people a little more civilised than the good Amlwchians.'

The dust and grime has disappeared, and today's 'Amlwchians' are no more unruly than the inhabitants of any other Anglesey town. The little harbour has lost its trading vessels, but still retains its atmosphere and has been landscaped to provide a pleasant place on a fine summer's day.

Directions:
From Holyhead, the A5 to Valley, then left along the A5025. Signs for Amlwch Port lead down to the small harbour, and then out to Llaneilian and Point Lynas.

Amlwch Port

Harnessing the Wind

Today's children associate windmills with the huge concrete stanchions crowning the hilltops, as in the north of Anglesey, their 'sails' turning constantly in the wind, which never seems to abate completely in this exposed part of the island.

Anglesey has always been at the mercy of the wind. But Anglesey people have recognised its use, too, and have harnessed it over the centuries to help grind corn.

At one time the island produced more grain than any other part of Wales. During the 16th and 17th centuries, windmills were built to cope with the increasing demand for grain as the population rose. Water mills could no longer cope, especially during dry summers when streams were reduced to a trickle and would be useless for turning heavy water wheels. Wind power, they found, was more dependable than water power.

There were, at one time, over forty working windmills on Anglesey. Some of them remain today, most of them sorry remnants of an industry which once flourished.

The pattern of farming on the island changed with the development of new forms of transport, which meant that cattle could be transported more easily. As a result, less demand accounted for fewer millwrights being trained. Gradually the mills ceased to operate, and became mere landmarks. Storms damaged many of them, and expensive repairs could not be undertaken.

Melin Llynon at Llanddeusant was one of the last to operate. Built in 1775-6, this great stone tower with its huge sails was damaged by a storm in 1918, which finally ended the business. By the late 1930s, Melin Llynon had fallen into disrepair. Nature did a good job. A storm destroyed the cap and most of the sails, and all that was left was the shell of the building, the cast-iron windshaft, and the cross.

Social historians realised that if Melin Llynon could not be saved, there would be little left on the island to show one of its most important industries of the past. In 1978 Anglesey Borough Council agreed to buy and restore it, and it is now one of the most popular tourist attractions on the island. And it continues to grind corn.

Llynon Mill

One of the few millwrights of high repute left in the country, M. Thompson & Son of Alford, Lincolnshire, was called in to assess the possibility of restoration. They suggested that bringing the old mill back to life could be done in three stages. Stage one was carried out at the company's works in Lincolnshire, which involved making the wooden curb in which the cap and sails would revolve, the frame to centre the cap and the upright shaft. Stage two began in 1982, when the oak frame to carry the cap was put in place. Once the cap was fitted, the mill was weatherproof and work could continue inside the building, to lay floors and to make the outside doors.

The final stage, undertaken in the spring of 1983, included fitting the internal machinery and four new sails. The sails were made at Alford, and by August had been delivered to Llanddeusant where, it is said, the whole village turned out to watch the assembly, and the day took on a carnival atmosphere.

On May the 11th, 1984, Melin Llynon, in full working order, was officially opened and the plaque now in place on the upended millstone at the entrance records the event.

Wind power was used for other industrial purposes, as at the copper works on Mynydd Parys, Amlwch, where the windmill pumped water from the copper workings below. The shell still remains, a landmark which can be seen from most parts of the island on a clear day.

Paint was made as a by-product, manufactured at the St Eilian Colour Works. A windmill was used to crush the yellow ochre and other coloured basic materials.

The Tan-yr-Efail windmill at Kingsland, Holyhead, supplied power to a sawmill and joinery works, belonging to a firm of builders below the rock on which it stood.

Of the forty mills whose sails turned in the strong Anglesey winds when grain was the most important industrial activity on Anglesey, all except Llynon Mill have disappeared, lie derelict with their sails long gone, or have been converted into unique houses.

Directions:
Melin Llynon is at Llanddeusant, approached by country roads from the A5025 between Llanynghenedl and Llanfaethlu. The mill stands prominently and can be seen over a wide area, making navigation towards it simple.

An 18th Century Diarist

Llanfechell is a small, somnolent village, away from any tourist route, lying in quiet green countryside south of Cemaes. The centre of the village is dominated by the parish church of St Mechell, standing in a venerable graveyard fringed with age-old yew trees. Close by stands Brynddu, a manor house, once the home of the 18th century squire, William Bulkeley, whose diaries give a vivid picture of life in Anglesey in his day.

William was 43 years old when he began to write his diary. There is no indication as to what inspired him to begin. His was the life typical of a squire of his time.

He saw to his estate, suffered money problems, and took relaxation in reading the work of Welsh poets. He worried about his family – he had two children, Mary and William, his wife having died on the birth of his son. He owned property in Ireland and travelled there to stay with his cousin. Family and country life and pursuits were his main occupations. William Bulkeley belonged to the lesser hierarchy of the Anglesey upper class, who had few financial resources and little inclination to curry favour in England. They were called, with a certain amount of scorn, 'the stay-at-home Welsh gentry'.

The garden at Brynddu was William's delight. He bought trees in Dublin; English elm, and apple trees of various kinds; dwarf box for edging borders; and currant trees for the walled garden. Farming was a necessary interest, as it provided a source of income. At the end of every harvest he would write: 'I praised God Almighty who gave seasonable weather for ripening the corn, and health to the inhabitance of the Island to get it in.'

He was a man of some local standing: he was a Juror at the Great Sessions held twice a year at Beaumaris, a Justice of the Peace at the Quarter Sessions, and served for a time as High Sheriff. His diary casts light on the way criminals were dealt with in the 18th century, and the harsh sentences pronounced.

An old woman from Llangaffo was charged with stealing forty shillings. She was sentenced to be 'burnt in the hand', as was the miller found guilty of manslaughter. This was a common occurrence, the sentence being carried out in court. John Pritchard, accused of burglary and felony, was condemned to be hanged.

There was one offence viewed with special leniency by the court, however. In his diary, honest William admitted: 'We are naturally reluctant to enforce the law against smugglers, when we all openly buy smuggled goods ourselves.'

William Bulkeley's children were to cause him great distress. His son, also named William, became a clerk to a lawyer in Chancery Lane, London. William regularly sent him money, to see him safely through the Inns of Court. That money was carried by a drover taking cattle to London.

He planned for young William to marry the eldest daughter of the Lloyd family of Llwydiarth, another Anglesey estate, hoping, by so doing, to reinforce his own finances. But his diary records:

> 'My boy never took the least freedom with the eldest, but the youngest I believe he did sometimes ogle and looked wishfully upon, which could be no disparagement at all to her or her father to have such alliance if he had really courted her in form. But ye old man I believe was afraid of ye Heiress who I believe would have received his addresses if he had made any advances that way, but he seemed to be wholly taken up in his thought with the youngest.'

Nothing came of the hoped for attachment however, and young William returned to London,

> 'Indulging himself in an indolent, sluggish way with very ordinary tipplers . . . and rakeing his way back to the city . . . time may bring him to be sensible of the wrong he does his character, and shame him to a reformation.'

Anglesey saw less and less of the young man as time passed, and his father only heard from him when he needed money.

'He had distressed me greatly. But he WAS my son for all that,' he wrote.

When William the younger died, William Bulkeley wrote sadly 'I did all I could in his last hours. He was brought to Llanfechell and buried in his mother's grave there. But need I say that my hopes for my son had been buried long since before that day.'

Mary, William Bulkeley's daughter, also caused him problems by marrying Fortunatus Wright, a Liverpool brewer and distiller. This followed a swift courtship while Mary was on holiday with William's cousin in Dublin. William made the best of what he considered an unfortunate match, and entertained Fortunatus and his heavily pregnant bride at Brynddu for some weeks on their return from Ireland. Mary miscarried shortly after, the first of several she was to suffer during her married life.

From then, Mary was subjected to what William described as 'barbarous usage and insults'. Fortunatus again sailed to Ireland, leaving Mary to suffer yet another miscarriage following ill-treatment by her husband.

Soon after, we hear of Fortunatus Wright being imprisoned in Italy, having been captured at sea. This suggested he had turned to privateering, and it became apparent that he led a double life, combining legitimate trade with piracy. Mary joined him in Italy, her two elder children remaining in Anglesey to receive their education in Beaumaris at William's expense. William even found himself paying interest on loans raised by his son-in-law.

After more cruel treatment, Mary sailed home, but was shipwrecked off the coast of Cornwall, rescued, and eventually went home to live the rest of her life at Brynddu. She was a disillusioned and unhappy woman, and poor company for her father who, by this time, was aged 68.

William's comment, 'The financial burden of my daughter's unfortunate life cost me dear,' said it all.

Apart from his family problems, William's diary records more pleasant topics, such as socialising in Beaumaris during the Great Sessions where he would meet up with his cronies. He had a keen interest in football which, in those days, was played on a Sunday or to mark a church festival. In the 18th century, football appeared to have few boundaries, with twelve men kicking a ball between two neighbouring parishes. A game could last three or four hours. One game between Llanfechell and Llanbadrig in 1743 had to be terminated as 'the football was driven over the precipice at Borth Badrick'.

William Bulkeley's allegiance to the church was strong throughout his life, but this did not prevent his criticising the quality of the sermons he heard. Parsons, he reflected, often gave 'dry, insipid discourses, trifling and pedantic'. On Easter Day, 1741, he wrote 'the priest was a very incoherent, unintelligible bombast'.

Brynddu, a gracious old house in a peaceful setting, retains its atmosphere of 18th century gentility, no doubt a remnant of the days when William Bulkeley was squire. It is not open to the public, but can be glimpsed through the trees.

Directions:

The minor road to Llanfechell leaves the A5025 between Tregele and Llanrhuddlad, and is signposted. William Bulkeley's diary is part of the Henblas Mss. at Bangor University Library. *Mr Bulkeley and the Pirate* by B. Dewi Roberts also tells his story.

Signal Station, Llaneilian

A Signal Success

When ships sail towards Liverpool today, their approach off the Anglesey coast is notified to the port by the most up to date methods of communication. In the days when tall ships were a frequent sight off Anglesey, communications were unsophisticated but ingenious.

In the early 1700s, Liverpool was a thriving port and many merchant ships used it. If you were a ship-owner in those days, living in the elegant new villas above the Mersey, a telescope was an essential part of your household furnishings. You would use it to scan the river for your home-coming ships, and to read messages conveyed by your house flag, one of many hoisted on the Bidston Hill flag poles to inform you of when your vessel was approaching port.

From Bidston Hill, a look-out could see far out into Liverpool Bay on a clear day. At one time there were around 100 poles, and signals from them were received by a watchman in Liverpool. The first lookout post was in a warehouse in Chapel Street, and later in the tower of St Nicholas's church. Messages were then rushed by runners to the nearby merchants' coffee houses.

In 1825 an Act of Parliament authorised the Liverpool Dock Trustees to 'establish a speedy mode of communication to the ship owners and merchants at Liverpool of the arrival of ships and vessels off the Port of Liverpool on the coast of Wales, by building, erecting and maintaining signal houses, telegraphs or such other modes of communication as to them shall seem expedient between Liverpool and Hoylake or between Liverpool and the Isle of Anglesea.'

After surveying, it was proposed that there should be 11 signal stations in the chain. Operators were to have a clear view to the previous station and to the next along the line.

The first site suggested was at Holyhead, between North and South Stack, about 500 ft above sea level. This station would pick up flag signals from passing ships, and relay them to the next station at Church Bay by semaphore.

About 10 miles east of Church Bay, over-looking Point Lynas lighthouse, surveyors marked the Llaneilian station. This was especially important because it was where the Mersey pilots took over to enter Liverpool, and where they were dropped as ships left the Bay.

Some 13 miles from Llaneilian is Ynys Seiriol. If ever there were an inhospitable, lonely site for a signal station, this was it. It was though ideally situated to pass on signals from Llaneilian to the next in line, on the top of the Great Orme at Llandudno.

Further stations were planned along the North Wales coast: at Llysfaen; Foryd on the River Clwyd; and Golden Grove behind Prestatyn. From there, messages passed to Hilbre Island and then to Bidston. The total distance was 72 miles.

Messages were relayed by semaphore, using identical masts at each station. Each was a tall pole with a top mast set above cross trees. The semaphore arms were painted black so that they could be seen clearly.

Strict rules were laid down for the operation of the system. The rule book warned operators 'All frivolous or useless communication should be avoided as it can tend to no good purpose and may occupy the telegraph when intelligence of importance at some other part of the line is waiting to be communicated.'

Operators became adept. Messages were sent by groups of numbers. An experienced operator could send them so rapidly that sometimes the first group of numbers would have arrived at Liverpool by the time the last was leaving Holyhead. Contact with the ships was by means of flags. Nine different colours were used, and they all worked to a similar code.

As soon as the system proved itself, improvements were made. The Church Bay station was augmented by a new one at Cefn Du, near Llanrhuddlad, so that one could be used if the other was shrouded in mist.

More substantial buildings were erected, all similar in style. Each house had four living rooms with a common chimney, and a bay windowed observation room. They were stone built, with slate roofs. Of the four Anglesey stations and one on Ynys Seiriol, only the Cefn Du building remains, and that is now a private house.

Directions:
Llanrhuddlad lies between Llanfaethlu and Cemaes Bay, on the A5025. The one-time signal station, has been named 'Craig y Gwynt', and bears a commemorative plaque which reads 'Cefn Du Telegraph Built in 1841 by the Trustees of the Liverpool Docks'.

A 19th C. Anglesey Childhood

Hidden behind trees in the undulating farmland between Bodedern and Llanynghenedl stands the old farmhouse of Mynydd-y-Gof. There is no plaque to commemorate the family who lived there in the middle of the 19th century, but one of the sons, Robert Roberts, wrote an account of his early days in Anglesey, and in so doing put Mynydd-y-Gof on the map.

Robert Roberts's father, David, was established at Mynydd-y-Gof before he married, being a gentleman farmer with a bailiff to run his farm. He also had an army of servants and labourers, while he carried on the profession of 'surgeon'. Robert calls him 'a duly licensed practitioner'.

David Roberts was a staunch Welsh Calvinistic Methodist, and made a practice of attending society and sessional meetings of the denomination. He once attended such a meeting in Aberystwyth and was given accommodation at the home of Simon and Sarah Lloyd at Machynlleth, where he met their daughter, Sarah, whom he later married. They had 10 children.

Robert's early recollections of his home were of a cheerful house, whitewashed from basement to roof, standing in the middle of a group of tall trees, shrubberies, and a large garden. There was a small paddock enclosed by a ha-ha.

David Roberts was a strict disciplinarian, with little sympathy for children at play. Robert wrote

> 'Although my father could be tolerant, and was tolerant in his views as regards hunting and field sports in general, he could be very different in regard to games of all sorts, such as football out of doors and all games of cards indoors.'

The children were not allowed to mix with the children of the village, although they were allowed to play with the bailiff's children. Dr Roberts had no interest in music, unless it was to accompany hymn singing in chapel. The family rose before six, summer and winter, and went to bed soon after eight o'clock in the evening.

The thread running through their lives was their religion. The children were taught to read by their mother, and what better primer, she believed, than the Bible which continued their religious instruction at the same time. Winter and summer alike, there was a daily session of Bible-reading, with each member of the family taking a verse at a time. The children had to attend all the chapel meetings, on Sundays and week-days, from a very early age.

Sunday morning prayers were a ritual at Mynydd-y-Gof. There would be quite a gathering in the kitchen when the family came in from the parlour after breakfast. When Robert's mother took her seat on a little rocking chair in front of the fireplace, little straw mats were placed before the chairs of the family, for the kitchen floor was stone-flagged and would be cold to the knees during long prayers. One solitary candle in addition to the light from the fire was all the light there was. It would be early, around half past six, so as to allow time to go to the morning prayer meeting at chapel, which was a good half an hour's walk from Mynydd-y-Gof, and which began at nine o'clock.

In this subdued light, all would be seated in perfect order and silence, awaiting the entrance of Robert's father. At length the door would open and he would make his dignified entrance.

> 'My father,' wrote Robert, 'always a striking figure, was dark, spare, and somewhat under the middle size, still a very erect figure. His hair black and smoothed down to half the forehead. His dress always black with a substantial silk bandana round his neck almost concealing the white stand-up collar. But the most remarkable thing in his appearance was the radiancy of countenance which impressed all that he was conscious of the dignity of the office as high priest in his own family. With serious mien he would walk to the table where the large family Bible was placed beside the candle and, seating himself on the chair, he would say to the bailiff, 'Well, Robin, will you begin?' '

Then members of the family and the servants, in turn, would recite verses. Some managed to commit chapters to memory, others, like Betty Hughes the serving maid, usually had to be prompted. Then followed a long prayer, with the children becoming restless yet trying not to show it for fear of reprimand. Robert recalls that towards the end, the candle would splutter in its socket and the fire burn low in the grate, while the day slowly dawned.

When the children had time to themselves, they would go birds-nesting, or bathe in the river in the summer. There was a sandhill at the farm, which provided some amusement, and there are constant references in Robert's account to trees, plants and flowers and descriptions of the marsh which edged the Mynydd-y-Gof farmland.

But it was not all paradise. He makes sad comment on the speed with which a family could be attacked by sickness in those days. One day he was playing with the bailiff's children, and the next day he and his brothers were forbidden to approach the cottage, as one of the children had contracted scarlet fever. She died quickly, to be followed by her sister a week later.

Outings were rare, but Robert does describe a visit he made with the servant, Betty, to her parents. They were desperately poor and lived on the Amlwch road on the far side of the marsh. Although almost destitute, he conveys the atmosphere of quiet dignity with which they received him. Another time he describes is a trip to the windmill at Llanfachraeth to fetch flour. Such simple outings, but red-letter days to a child whose lifestyle was restricted.

Visitors to the house were also rare, except for family who arrived by horse and gig. Robert looked forward to these visits beacause it meant that the usual Bible reading was suspended, and his mother would kill a fowl and they enjoyed chicken and pancakes for supper. Meals were plain but wholesome. There was usually a good meat supper after chapel on Sunday – it was probably well deserved after three enforced attendances at services during the day.

We are given a glimpse of stiff Victorian manners through Robert's reference to conversation between his mother and father. Although subservient to her husband in most things, his mother could on occasions reprimand him quietly. She did not approve of discussing religion in company, and after David Roberts had done so, she would say to him 'I wish you had not introduced the subject you did, Mr Roberts bach.'

Throughout the first chapters of Robert Roberts's story of his family, he returns frequently to the part religion played in their lives.

The family attended Capel Mawr in the village, dimly lit by home-made candles fixed to a piece of wood and fastened to the walls between three nails. A few candles were also placed on the backs of the pews. The chapel had no ceiling, and shadows flickered eerily among the rafters.

> 'Anything more dismal than the singing, the reading and the prayer cannot be imagined,' he wrote.

The monthly meetings where chapel members paid their contributions shortened the prayer meeting, and were welcomed by the children, who watched the congregation process to the front of the chapel to pay their pennies, twopences and threepences to his father.

Anyone committing the sin of adultery, or even drunkenness, was liable to be banished from the chapel society. This would be done with awful solemnity in the presence of the congregation. Robert describes one such event, when his father decreed that all the children must attend, as 'it was the duty and privilege of children to witness the administration of an ordinance of the church for their edification.'

We read about the plight of the clergy in Anglesey, some having to undertake other work to supplement their meagre income. Field preaching was all the vogue. Sunday games and cock-fighting had largely disappeared, but many farmers and servants did not attend a place of worship. It was with the idea of gathering them into the fold that field-preaching was encouraged. The pulpit was nothing more than a cart and some planks, and if it rained some obliging local sailor would provide sails as a covering. And how the children would look forward to this change to their normally boring Sunday.

Those who knew Manchester in the early and mid-20th century will no doubt recall the great warehouse of J.F. & H. Roberts in the city centre. It was a mecca for Welsh drapers who, once or twice a year, came to Manchester to replenish their stocks. This was the family business which made a comfortable living for the Roberts sons as they became adults and moved to live in the city.

Robert Roberts's life style has long since disappeared, but Mynydd-y-Gof still stands testimony to one old way of life in rural Anglesey.

Directions:
Mynydd-y-Gof lies across the fields and in a copse of trees, on the B5109, mid-way between Bodedern and Llanynghenedl. It is privately owned. There is a copy of Robert Roberts's memoirs at the Llangefni Library local history collection.

Thespians in Llangefni

The campus of Coleg Menai in Llangefni occupies the one-time Pencraig estate on the edge of the town. As well as being an important branch of this exceptionally busy college of further education, it is also the home of 'Y Theatr Fach', a little theatre.

The Llangefni Drama Society was set up in 1949. It was the dream-child of George Fisher, mathematics master at the Llangefni Grammar School, and a native of Maesteg in Glamorgan. Although originally monoglot English, he learnt Welsh so thoroughly that he won three drama composition prizes at successive National Eisteddfodau. Throughout his life, literature was at the centre of his many interests and accomplishments. George Fisher was the Society's first secretary.

The Society rehearsed their plays at the Grammar School, and as their collection of sets and props grew, they were given permission to house them all in an empty swimming pool. In 1954 they were given notice to quit, as the building was to be demolished.

Fortune was on their side. The local authority decided to buy Pencraig and 100 acres of land surrounding it. The Society immediately focussed its attention on the stables, with a view to buying and converting the rundown building into a small theatre.

This they did, first renting at five shillings a week, and then buying the property for £250 – a small sum as the council recognised and supported their aims. The stables looked reasonable from the outside, but inside was a different story.

Twenty-five volunteers moved in to restore the building, and in three months, it was ready for use. It was capable of seating an audience of 60. The official opening took place on May the 3rd 1955. By 1957, the theatre capacity had been extended to hold 112.

A reflection on the high standard of production came in 1962 when the Society became a member of the Society of Small Theatres of Britain. At the time, twenty-six groups were members, only three of them in Wales. In 1983, when a history of the Society was written, 'Y Theatr Fach' was the only theatre staging plays in Welsh and English.

Many renowned Welsh actors of stage and television received their grounding at 'Y Theatr Fach'.

Directions:
'Y Theatr Fach' can be approached through the entrance to Coleg Menai, Pencraig Site. It is a little way out of Llangefni, on the Llangefni-Penmynydd-Menai Bridge road.

Theatr Fach Llangefni

The Misses Massey of Cornelyn

In addition to the famous collection of pictures by C.F. Tunnicliffe at Oriel Ynys Môn, Llangefni, is a valuable record of Anglesey's botanical history made by two sisters: Edith Ellen Henrietta and Gwendoline Elizabeth Eveleen Massey. The collection of around 500 pictures was bought at auction at Christie's, by the then Ynys Môn Borough Council, for £2,000. They were painted during the 1920s and 1930s, one sister specialising in pencil drawing and the other in water colour painting. The Massey home was Cornelyn Manor, Llangoed, which is no longer a private house. But much of their work was done in a cottage on the shore near Penmon, where they would spend a fortnight at a time during the summer.

It is believed that the sisters came to Anglesey from Cheshire, where their parents had a connection with Puddington Hall on the Wirral. They had two brothers, although only one appears to have spent any time in Anglesey.

As with many other moneyed families of the early 1900s, they moved in their own social circle, rubbing shoulders with the local aristocracy and gentry. They hunted, they travelled, and they attended all the social functions where it was good policy to be seen. The sisters not only drew and painted, but also enjoyed needlework. A retainer who remembered them at Cornelyn recalled that they made the lace for the maids' uniform caps, to be worn when on duty in the house.

Gwendoline kept two scrapbooks, now in the archives of the University of Wales at Bangor. She wrote them in a large, clear hand, in black ink on white boards which were bound together to form two large volumes. These are full of drawings and photographs of local people and places. One deals solely with the Anglesey Hunt. This volume is prefaced with a large photograph of Gwendoline's sister, Edith, dressed in green riding habit, a bowler with a face veil, and a bunch of violets in her coat lapel below her stock pin. She stands by her horse.

All the local hunts are recorded, along with anecdotes and memories of hunting personalities, such as the Rev. John Owen of Llaneilian who owned a pack of foot harriers in 1837. He would hunt twice a week in the country around Amlwch, dressed in clerical attire and a big white cravat.

Sometimes the local farmers would be invited to hunt with him. They all sat down to dinner at five o'clock after a day in the field, to be enlivened by an old harper.

But the main attraction of these two volumes is their decoration. Gwendoline illuminated the capitals, and a riot of country animals tumble down the margins and across the foot of the pages. She used gold leaf abundantly. Her foxes and rabbit for example are all gold, and have riveting red glass eyes.

Directions:

Oriel Ynys Môn stands to one side of the B5111 north of Llangefni. The University College Archives office is in the main University building. Requests to see archives should be made by telephone prior to visiting. No reader's card is necessary. Telephone: 01248 382966.

Ynys Seiriol

To visitors other than Welsh, the small island off the eastern tip of Anglesey is known as Puffin Island. But its true name is Ynys Seiriol, after the early saint who established a monastic settlement there during the 6th century.

The island saw another use during the 19th century, when it was the site of one of the telegraph stations from which messages were relayed to ships as they approached Holyhead, on their way to Liverpool. This was part of a semaphore system, an astonishingly successful and rapid way of transmitting messages to and from Liverpool on a clear day.

Ynys Seiriol is not usually accessible to the public, without prior permission. It was once famous for its colony of puffins, but rats and a one-time partiality for pickled puffins led to their disappearance. But the island is still the home of many sea-birds who nest on its rocky cliffs, and boat trips from Beaumaris in fine weather allow visitors to view from off-shore.

The recipe book of Margaret Wynne, Boderwyd, now at the Anglesey Archives office in Llangefni, gives a recipe to pickle puffins.

> 'Make ye puffins cleane as soon as you take ym & draw them yn let ym lye in water & salt a whole night. Yn wash yn clean in yt liquor and turn up there leggs and parboyle ym in water and salt for halfe an houre and as you take ym out of ye hott water shake ym in cold water, and sett ym endwaies to run all night. Next morning lay them flat on there breast in a dry cloth and crush them a little till they be thoroughly dry, yn scrape ym clean with a knife and lay ym on there brests in ye vessel.
>
> Then take a pottle of white wine and as much white wine venegar and 2 potties of Alagar, 2 mace, ginger & 2 peper, ye mace and peper must be brused, ye ginger sliced, yn boyle all these a litle in ye liquor with a handfull of salt and when it is throughly cold cleare it and take ye spice yt is in ye bottom and throw between every lay of ye puffins in ye vessell as you pack ym up in ye liquor and put a round slate or board to keep ym under water and stop up ye vessel close yt no wind gett in. This liquor and spice is a fitt proportion for 6 dozen.'

Puffin

Directions:

The closest point to Ynys Seiriol on the landward side is Trwyn Du. To reach Penmon, drive to Beaumaris then continue eastwards along the coast for four miles. There is parking outside the Priory. By paying a toll, it is possible to continue further along the private road from the Priory to Trwyn Du, where there is parking space on the shore.

Read All About It

Today several locally published newspapers on Anglesey give a local news service, some entirely in Welsh. In the early 19th century, when Wellington was taking his army into Spain, the North Wales Gazette appeared for the first time. It was a news-sheet intended to appeal to the comparatively few English readers living in North Wales in 1808. It trod warily with the first few issues, obviously trying to impress its readers with an aura of solidarity and wisdom as far as the more serious problems of the age were concerned. Its main purpose, however, was to spread local news. There were no illustrations. The type was small. But what the North Wales Gazette of 1808 lacked in visual presentation, it made up with turn of phrase and local interest.

It carried a 'Births, Marriages and Deaths' column. When Owen Williams married Margaret Parry, the notice read

> 'Marriage: Monday, Owen Williams of the Parish of Llanwenllwyfo to Margaret Parry of the Parish of Amlwch. He is aged 88 and the fourth husband to the bride; and she is 60 and the third wife to the bridegroom. The bride's late husband and the bridegroom's late wife were interred within the last 18 months.'

A comment which followed another notice of marriage was enough to bring a blush to the cheek of the bride:

> 'On Sunday sen'night,' it read, 'Mr Ed. Bignall to Miss Wilson, and on the following morning the blooming bride presented her lord and master with a fine boy. For a moment we hesitated whether the birth or marriage ought to be honoured with this article, but we determined that marriage ought, in all propriety, to take the precedency.'

Crime was rife in 1808, but sentences were out of all proportion to their severity.

> 'John Pritchard was charged at the Beaumaris Assizes before Hugh Leycester, Esq., and Sir Thomas Plommer, Knight, judges for these districts, with stealing a quantity of cordage, with part of which he

made a ladder of ropes which he conveyed down the chimney of the library of the Rev. Lewis of Llanrhyddlad and stole thereout upwards of 40 volumes of books. He was convicted and sentenced to be sent on board a man of war for a course of life which he did not seem to approve of, as he escaped from his prison soon after his sentence was made known to him.'

Advertisements of the day were to the point, although some of them were lengthy. Under a 'Lost or Found' heading appears

'Whereas on Tuesday, June 14, 1808, was sent from Beaumaris a brown paper parcel to be forwarded per packet from the Bangor Ferry containing two wide twill'd cambric shawls, two silk borders ditto and seven yards fine cotton diaper, which said parcel is not yet arrived. Whoever will give intelligence of it shall receive half a guinea reward by offering to Mr Jackson, Bangor Ferry or to William Jackson, draper, Beaumaris. If the above goods should be exposed for sale or secreted, whoever will give the information which may lead to the discovery shall receive a reward of two guineas.'

Two guineas was a fortune in those days. Did Mr Jackson, the draper of Beaumaris, ever recover his parcel?

Directions:
The Anglesey archives office in the Old Council Office in Glanhwfa Road, Llangefni carries early issues of some local newspapers. These can be referred to without prior booking.

The Court House, Beaumaris

Grace Garth The Ferrywoman

Before the two bridges were built across the Menai Strait, and for some time after, five ferries plied from Caernarfonshire to Anglesey. One of the busiest of these was the Garth Ferry, which operated across the narrowest part of the Strait.

In the latter part of the 18th century, the ferry was worked by a country woman named Grace Parry. She was described in a diary as 'a short, thick, squat female who, though upwards of sixty winters have passed over her head, is as strong as a horse and as active as one of her own country goats. Her excellence in rowing and manning a boat leaves nothing to be desired.'

Apparently 'Gras-y-Garth', as she was called, inherited this aptitude from her parents, who had looked after the ferry for a life-time before her. She was brought up among the boats. Her father was a particularly strong swimmer, and when he and her mother manned the boat together they would not always agree. The old lady was the better of the two when it came to an argument and sometimes, unable to bear it, Parry would suddenly cast off his jacket, leap into the water and swim across towards his cottage, shouting back abuse at his wife.

Grace Parry carried much of her mother's spirit and looked down severely on the opposite sex. She was married, but never allowed her husband to row and fish with her – because he could not row and fish half as well as she could!

Her prejudices against the English were violent, especially when she was under the influence of drink, but a double tip would dispel them completely!

The diarist records how she shook hands with him and his party when they landed. Whether she meant it as a token of goodwill or proof of strength he could not say, as she almost dislocated their fingers in her grip.

When you make your comfortable crossing on to Anglesey, give a thought to the perils of the past, and Grace Parry and her cockleshell boat.

There are few remains to indicate the positions of most of the old ferries.

Topcoat for the Turnkey

Today, footsteps echo with a hollow sound as visitors walk the stone passages past the yard where prisoners once took their exercise at Beaumaris Gaol. The treadmill is now still.

A collection of record books exists, compiled in the prison during the latter half of the 19th century, and giving a glimpse of prison life long ago.

It appears that prisoners were committed to Beaumaris Prison for larceny, burglary, acts of nuisance and for not fulfilling work contracts. When they arrived at the gaol, particulars were taken of their weight and personal possessions in the Prisoners' Property Book. The entries were made in neat script and meticulously ruled columns. Articles of clothing listed were a coat, 'trowsers', vest, shirt, under-shirt, boots (few had these), shoes, stockings, hat, cap, handkerchief, drawers, braces and clogs. The column for 'extra articles' varied from a stick to a tin trunk.

One prisoner named John Read, in 1857, had the misfortune to be 'labouring under an itch', and the records state briefly that his clothing was 'kept separate'.

The Misconduct Book for 1849 makes fascinating reading.

A 14-years old boy, Ralph Williams, was confined for two days in a solitary cell, on bread and water, for 'cursing, swearing and other misdemeanors'. George Smith, aged 23, had three days in the punishment cell on bread and water for concealing a sledge hammer in his clothes, and taking it to his cell 'with intent to either murder or breaking the iron bars of his bed cell'. Elizabeth Wakefield objected loudly to having to attend chapel, and was sentenced to three days in the solitary cell for 'irreverent behaviour'. But on the order of the surgeon, she was moved to the day room as she was subject to fits.

Many prisoners had their meals stopped because they were insolent, and refusal to work incurred several days' close confinement in handcuffs. Meals were stopped, too, if prisoners climbed over their airing-yard walls to talk to other prisoners, and there is a record of a boy, Owen Davies, who refused to get out of bed and so had to forfeit his dinner.

Another boy, Evan Pierce, spent twenty-four hours in the punishment cell for stealing tobacco from the pocket of a workman employed in the gaol.

The names of prisoners who were taken ill and whose diets had to be altered accordingly were entered in the Extra Diet Book. A prisoner named Holden was to have bread and butter and milk for dinner every day, and a ration of four ounces of brandy each day for three days. Two days later the record suggests he must have recovered, for the entry reads 'to have a chop for his dinner, and to continue the brandy for three days longer.' Drinks instead of the usual gruel were sometimes ordered for certain prisoners, usually coffee without milk, cocoa, tea or milk.

On April the 19th, 1864, a prisoner named Pritchard was to have two ounces of arrowroot in milk and two ounces of sherry, with the warning and restrictive adjunct 'today only'. May McNally was prescribed twelve ounces of treacle weekly, and Macdonald, obviously a sick man, had his rations altered three times in one month. He was given extra bread and beef, with the instruction that the beef had to be made into a mash.

Perhaps the saddest reflection on the times was the entry for Bridget Reilly in 1868. She had been sentenced to two months' hard labour for larceny, and her baby was in prison with her. In June of that year she was prescribed two ounces of tea, half a pound of sugar and half a pound of butter weekly; then later, a pound of sugar a week, and a pint of milk daily for the baby. Her health must have declined slowly, for the next entry in July, ordered her to have two pints of milk a day, a pint of porter and an egg.

Prisoners' weight on leaving was also recorded in the Prisoners' Property Book, and it is interesting to note that all, without exception, left some weight behind them in Beaumaris Gaol. The prisoners' life was hard, but the working days of those who ran the prison must have been anything but pleasant.

In winter, Beaumaris Gaol was a cold, dank place. Reading the Quarter Sessions records for 1866, we can sympathise with the plight of the turnkey who applied for more clothes. The record states briefly, and grudgingly, 'the clothing of the latter for the year to include a Top Coat – but not every year'.

Directions:
Beaumaris Gaol in Steeple Lane, to the side of St Mary's Church, is open to the public. A leaflet is available from Tourist Information Centres and libraries, giving details.

The Gaol, Beaumaris

The Last Execution

There is no stone to show the burial place of Dic Rolant, but notoriety has preserved his memory over the years.

It was in 1862 that Richard Rowlands, a labourer more familiarly known as Dic Rolant, was accused of murdering his father-in-law. He had married a widow, the daughter of Richard Williams who farmed at Garnedd, Llanfaethlu in north Anglesey. Williams was against the marriage and refused to let Dic make his home at Garnedd. He was allowed to visit his wife during the day, but had to return to his parents' home to sleep.

One evening, the old man left the farm and was found the next morning lying in a ditch. All the evidence pointed to a murder, and it was not long before Dic Rolant was arrested.

Special editions of the local paper featured the news, which was hailed with horror by readers. There were no bold, black headlines, but reporters played on the imagination of their readers with lurid, long drawn out descriptions which appealed to their emotions.

As a result of this publicity, when the court at Beaumaris opened to hear the case on March the 22nd, 1862, there was 'a great rush made to the doors which were almost carried by storm . . . the court was crammed in every part with well dressed persons and hundreds remained outside, unable to obtain permission.'

When Dic Rolant appeared in court, the newspapermen reported: 'His careworn appearance foretold the anxiety of mind under which he had laboured since his committal.' Nevertheless, he pleaded not guilty and held his plea even when the judge donned the black cap and pronounced his fate.

The press reported emphatically 'we may state on the authority of those to whom he was best known that his character through life was such as to render him an object to be shunned in society – dangerous alike to the innocence, the purity and the morals of those among whom he resided.'

The day of execution dawned. Never had Beaumaris seen such excitement. While carpenters from Chester erected the scaffold, which projected from the tall wall of the gaol in Steeple Lane, plans were being carried out to evacuate the children from the town, lest any should see the horror. The National school children were invited by Sir Richard Williams Bulkeley to spend the day in the grounds of nearby Baron Hill; and the Grammar School pupils were shipped to Aber, well out of the way.

The Garth Ferry boat, plying across the Strait to Bangor, did a busy trade with passengers from the mainland who wished to witness the hanging, and in the opposite direction, those who wanted to get away from it all. The roads to Beaumaris from all parts of the island were crammed with curious sightseers.

Beds in the town's guest houses were at a premium, and people living in the vicinity of the gallows made a small fortune by letting their front gardens at sixpence a time. Extra police were brought in to deal with any disturbance, and special constables were sworn in.

While all these preparations were being made, life inside the prison was reaching a high pitch of emotional stress. In vain, ministers of religion, from Beaumaris and elsewhere, pleaded with the condemned man to confess his crime, but Dic Rolant remained firm. His wife and children were brought to see him 'bathed in tears', and the newspapers reported their conversation in detail.

One feels, however, on reading the newspaper reports, that even the journalists who covered the story were by now being affected as their reports become almost sympathetic. We are invited to see Dic Rolant as a poor unfortunate, being pestered in the last hours of his life to admit to a crime he had not perpetrated. We are reminded that he never availed himself of special privileges while in prison, and had no additional diet.

On April the 4th, 1862, the crowd, gathered in front of the gallows, was not made up of the low riff-raff and scum of society as was often the case on such occasions. Instead, it numbered hundreds of well dressed and apparently well-to-do people. Here was a hanging with a difference. The services of the extra police were not needed, for the crowd was orderly and well behaved.

At eight o'clock in the morning, the door at the end of the passageway opened, and the party walked out of the cell of the condemned along the platform especially made, and out on to the scaffold. Dic Rolant shook hands with the executioner; the noose was fastened; the bolt drawn and 'the unhappy man was launched into eternity'.

Sensational to the last, the newspaper report goes on: 'A deeply suppressed groan was heard rising from the crowd below which was soon hushed into an awful silence. His death was instantaneous. His body, after hanging an hour, was cut down and placed in a shell and buried within the precincts of the gaol.'

So generations of visitors to Beaumaris have gazed on the burial place of the last man to be hung in Anglesey. Was he innocent? We shall never know.

Directions:
Beaumaris Court House at the eastern end of Castle Street was in use until the latter years of the 20th century. It is now open to visitors, as is the gaol in Steeple Lane. A video of a dramatic reconstruction of the trial has been produced by the Isle of Anglesey County Council, and is on sale at the Court House.

Requiescat in Pace

The present-day preference for cremation, rather than burial, means that tomorrow's historians are going to miss out on an important and fruitful source of information – gravestones and their epitaphs.

Today's burials are marked in a noncommittal way. No longer is it the fashion to include on a gravestone mention of the personal attributes of the deceased, what his occupation was, or how he died. Masons have no rich little tit-bits of detail or comment to incise. The more modern corners of our graveyards have become very impersonal places.

But old churchyards abound in Anglesey, and it is still possible to browse, and to get to know some of those laid to rest a century ago or more.

Take the churchyard on Church Island, below the Menai Suspension Bridge, for instance. Occasional thoughtful tidying and grass cutting makes inspection easier.

It is there that we meet Joseph Keeble, who died aged 78 in 1884, and 'was for many years a faithful and valued servant in the service of Captain and Mrs F. Mansel Morgan'. No doubt they stood, or at least contributed to, the cost of the memorial.

Others in domestic service, Mary and Robert Hughes, died in 1911 and are recorded on a tablet 'affectionately raised to two good and faithful servants by their old mistress, Georgina Weldon'.

There are memorials to those who died far away from Church Island. Like Ann Elizabeth Hughes who died in Williamstown, Australia, in 1856, at the early age of 29. She had a child of four, who died at the early age of 16. What was their story?

A glance at ages recorded on the memorials reminds one of the high rate of infant mortality in the middle 1800s. William Jones, Coroner for Anglesey, and his wife Hannah, buried five children aged between six months and ten years between 1859 and 1868.

Several epitaphs record tragic deaths. How did 14-years old Thomas, son of Henry Evans 'mariner of this parish and Anne his wife' meet his untimely death? The inscription says he was drowned in the Strait in

1872. Was he sailing through the treacherous Swillies? Or was he larking with others, and did his boat capsize?

William Price, 'Master Mariner of the city of Bangor' was drowned in Runcorn in 1852, the last place one would expect to be the scene of such a tragedy.

George Ellis Roberts of the Marquis Inn, Bangor, 'met his death by an accident while in the employ of the London North Western Railway Company' in 1876. What were the circumstances? Why was he buried at Church Island and not in Bangor?

The fashion for including the occupation of the deceased on a gravestone has disappeared. How much more interesting it is to read of a man who was 'an estate agent to the Duke of Manchester on his extensive Connemara estate, including various town lands'; or, as in the case of William Mason Crowther who died in August 1873, 'agent to the Bodelwyddan and Rhianva estates for 46 years'. A few words say so much.

We are reminded of the existence of many wrecks around the Anglesey coast by the burials which took place in the coastal churchyards.

The churchyard of St Gallgo's church at Llanallgo is the resting place of many whose bodies were washed ashore at Moelfre after being drowned in the wreck of the 'Royal Charter'. This happened during a severe storm in October, 1859, which accounted for more than 100 wrecks off the Anglesey coast. The ship was returning to Liverpool from Australia with a complement of over 400 passengers, many of them wealthy after prospecting for gold. It was said that around £370,000 worth of gold was scattered in the sea.

A memorial in the churchyard remembers the dead. An inscription on one of the stones reads:

> 'Sacred to the memory of George Edmund Farncomb Hatch, Surgeon of Farnham, Royal Bucks, who perished in the wreck of the *Royal Charter* on the morning of the 26th October, 1859 . . . He was a kind friend, father and husband, and his last moments were passed in cheering his companions in misfortune.'

Exactly 100 years later a 500-tonne Cardiff coaster, 'Hindlea' was wrecked off this coast, when eight of the crew were rescued.

The Lifeboat station at Moelfre is one of the most famous in Britain, its crew having saved hundreds of lives over a number of years.

Directions:

Church Island lies slightly west of, and below the Menai Suspension Bridge. Cars may be left at the Coed Cyrnol car park, opposite the police station on the road from the bridge towards Llanfairpwll. A path leads through the wood to the causeway linking Church Island with the mainland – it is accessible at all times.

Llanallgo Church is on the left hand side of the A5025 travelling from Benllech to Amlwch. It is half a mile from the roundabout where the A5108 leads to Moelfre.

Anglesey Titles

Titles of interest about Anglesey

ANGLESEY – AN ISLAND'S STORY
Michael Senior
ISBN: 0-86381-389-5; £2.75

ANGLESEY SKETCHES
Margaret Hughes; illustrations by N. Squire Johnson
ISBN: 0-86381-540-5; £3.95

ANGLESEY PAST AND PRESENT
Wendy Hughes
ISBN: 0-86381-560-X; £4.95

TWO BRIDGES OVER MENAI
Robin Richards
ISBN: 0-86381-387-9; £2.75

CIRCULAR WALKS ON ANGLESEY
Dorothy Hamilton
ISBN: 0-86381-478-6; £4.50

SHROUDED QUAYS – THE LOST PORTS OF WALES
Aled Eames
ISBN: 0-86381-197-3; £2.50

THE HERRING FISHERS OF WALES
Mike Smylie
ISBN: 0-86381-467-0; £3.75

AN ANGLESEY ANTHOLOGY
Dewi Roberts
ISBN: 0-86381-566-9; £4.95

Full catalogue and price list available from:
GWASG CARREG GWALCH,
12 Iard yr Orsaf, Llanrwst, Conwy, Wales, LL26 0EH.

Anglesey
PAST & PRESENT
Wendy Hughes

Circular Walks
on Anglesey

ANGLESEY
The Island's Story
Michael Senior
REVISED EDITION

Two Bridges over Menai
Robin Richards

Industrial Archaeology & Railways

A Gazeteer of the Welsh Slate Industry

– Alun John Richards. Details and historical notes on 400+ quarries and mills in Wales representing 20 years of field work.
240 pp; ISBN 0-86381-196-5; **£6.90**

Slate Quarrying in Wales

– Alun John Richards. From its earliest beginnings to the present day, this book follows the fortunes and misfortunes of this great industry.
231 pp; ISBN 0-86381-319-4; **£7.50**

Slate Quarrying in Corris

– Alun John Richards. First detailed account of the area.
144 pp; ISBN 0-86381-279-1; **£5.45**

Delving in Dinorwig

– Douglas C. Carrington. First detailed account of a fascinating slate quarry. ISBN 0-86381-285-6; **£7.50**

The Golden Age of Brymbo Steam

– Geoff and Hugh Charles. Old photographs and memories of the Brymbo railway lines. ISBN 0-86381-435-2; **£5.75**

Three Stops to the Summit

– Rol Williams. The history of the Snowdon Mountain Railway.
ISBN 0-86381-433-6; **£4.95**

Historic Landscapes of the Great Orme

– Mary Aris. Early agriculture and copper-mining – a new persepctive on Llandudno's landscape and history. 114 pages quarto; maps; diagrams; illustrations; ISBN 0-86381-357-7; **£7.95**

The Llŷn Peninsula Mines

– Wil Williams. A history of manganese mining on the peninsula; 64 pages; bilingual; illustrations. ISBN 0-86381-315-1; **£3**

New for 1998:

The Slate Quarries of Pembrokeshire

– Alun John Richards. Including illustrations & maps.
ISBN 0-86381-484-0; **£5.50**

Children's Books

STORIES FROM WALES

This series introduces some of our country's best-loved stories to a new generation, with plenty of eyecatching colour illustrations by Carys Owen.

1 **Gelert:** the faithful hound. ISBN 0-86381-392-5; **£3.50**
2 **Olwen:** the giant's daughter. ISBN 0-86381-393-3; **£3.50**
3 **The King's Ears:** a royal secret. ISBN 0-86381-394-1; **£3.50**
To be published September 1998: **The Lost Land; The Lady of the Lake; The Red Dragon of Wales.**

FOLK TALES FROM WALES

Retold by Siân Lewis, A4 format, full colour illustrations by Gini Wade; hard-back.

Cadog and The Mouse: A kind monk is helped by a mouse during a famine on the land. ISBN 0-86381-417-4; **£2.99**

Rhys and The Cuckoo of Risca: The people of Risca try to keep the cuckoo in their land through the winter. ISBN 0-86381-419-0; **£2.99**

Regions of Wales

'THE STORY OF . . .' Series

Wendy Hughes interweaves history, tales and events with attractive and interesting locations that will captivate and excite the visitor, leaving the reader breathless and surprised as she turns back the tide of time and glimpses into each century.

The Story of Gower. 88 pp; ISBN 0-86381-217-1; **£3.75**
The Story of Pembrokeshire. 100 pp; ISBN 0-86381-253-8; **£3.75**
The Story of Brecknock. 104 pp; ISBN 0-86381-316-X; **£4.25**

Radnorshire – A Historical Guide

– Donald Gregory. Radnorshire in many respects is Wales in a microcosm – hilly, wild, beautiful and small with the past ever present.
168 pp; 0-86381-284-8; **£4.50**

THE MICHAEL SENIOR SERIES – *A widely published historian with a series of well written volumes about different areas of North Wales.*

The Conwy Valley – Its Long History. 48 pp; ISBN 0-86381-035-7; **£1.50**
Llandudno's Story. 32 pp; ISBN 0-86381-391-7; **£1.75**
Anglesey – The Island's History. 64 pp; ISBN 0-86381-389-5; **£2.75**
Conwy – The Town's Story. 32 pp; ISBN 0-86381-345-3; **£1.95**
Caernarfon – The Town's Story. 32 pp; ISBN 0-86381-346-1; **£1.95**
Llŷn – The Peninsula's Story. 48 pp; full of illustrations; ISBN 0-86381-443-3; **£1.95**
Meirionnydd's Story. 64 pp; full of illustrations; ISBN 0-86381-442-5; **£1.95**

The Crossing of the Conwy

– Michael Senior. From prehistoric times to the new tunnel.
112 pp; ISBN 0-86381-191-4; **£3.75**

North Wales in the Making

– Michael Senior. A guide to the area's early history. Hard-back.
128 pp; ISBN 0-86381-322-4; **£9.75**

Two Bridges over Menai

– Robin Richards. History of the construction of the bridges across the Menai Straits. ISBN 0-86381-387-9; **£2.75**

This Valley was ours

– Eileen M. Webb. History of Nant Gwrtheyrn as remembered by one of the village's children. ISBN 0-86381- 428-X; **£7.50**

Place-names

Place-names of Dee and Alun

– Hywel Wyn Owen. 64 pp; ISBN 0-86381-325-9; **£3.75**

Place-names in the 3000ft Mountains of Wales

– Terry Batt. 180 pp; ISBN 0-86381-282-1; **£4.50**

A Guide to Welsh Place-names

– Anthony Lias. Over 500 examples giving meaning and analysing in a simple and concise way. 110 pp; ISBN 0-86381-289-9; **£3.50**

Cynon Valley Place-names

– Deric John. ISBN 0-86381-472-7; **£4.50**

Pronouncing Welsh Place-names

– Tony Leaver. Featuring Instant Guide to well-known names.
ISBN 0-86381-482-4; **£4.50**